Jean,

Enjoy the re
Not just for
entrepreneurs.

Delin

*For more from Del Chatterson's Uncle Ralph:*

Visit: LearningEntrepreneurship.com

*Or follow Del on:*

Facebook: https://www.facebook.com/YourUncleRalph
LinkedIn: http://ca.linkedin.com/in/delchatterson
Twitter: http://twitter.com/Del_UncleRalph
Blog for Entrepreneurs: e2eForum.com

*And to prepare a better Business Plan:*

**The Complete Do-It-Yourself Guide to Business Plans**
**"It's about the process, not the product"**
New, Revised and Expanded, Second Edition © 2014

Or visit: DIYBusinessPlan.com

# Don't Do It the Hard Way

*"A wise man learns from the mistakes of others,
Only a fool insists on making his own."*

*Your Uncle Ralph,* **Delvin R. Chatterson**

*AuthorHouse™*
*1663 Liberty Drive*
*Bloomington, IN 47403*
*www.authorhouse.com*
*Phone: 1-800-839-8640*

*© 2014 Your Uncle Ralph, Delvin R. Chatterson. All rights reserved.*

*No part of this book may be reproduced, stored in a retrieval system, or transmitted by any means without the written permission of the author.*

*Throughout this book, the actual names and business details have been changed to protect the subjects of each story. Any apparent use of real names is purely coincidental.*

*Published by AuthorHouse 9/3/2014*

*ISBN: 978-1-4969-3225-9 (sc)*
*ISBN: 978-1-4969-3224-2 (hc)*
*ISBN: 978-1-4969-3223-5 (e)*

*Library of Congress Control Number: 2014914069*

*Any people depicted in stock imagery provided by Thinkstock are models, and such images are being used for illustrative purposes only. Certain stock imagery © Thinkstock.*

*This book is printed on acid-free paper.*

*Because of the dynamic nature of the Internet, any web addresses or links contained in this book may have changed since publication and may no longer be valid. The views expressed in this work are solely those of the author and do not necessarily reflect the views of the publisher, and the publisher hereby disclaims any responsibility for them.*

*Dedicated to the principle that entrepreneurs who do better for themselves will also do better for their families, employees, customers and suppliers; their communities and the planet.*

*Do better.*

# Can I help you do better?

My intent is to share my knowledge and experience in entrepreneurship – how to start and run a successful business. We all learn from our mistakes, but it is also important to learn from the mistakes of others. We don't have to make them all ourselves – life is too short!

This book is based on the principle that entrepreneurs learn the most from other entrepreneurs and learn best by sharing stories. In each chapter I share my own stories, including the mistakes I have made, and the stories of other entrepreneurs who have also learned from their mistakes. Of course, I will also share what we have learned by occasionally getting it right.

Some of the most important lessons will help you with these challenges:

- *Getting Started*
  When and how? Can you succeed as an entrepreneur?

- *Strategic Leadership plus Operating Effectiveness*
  The biggest challenge for every entrepreneur is to provide strategic leadership while managing effectively.

- *Managing Relationships*
  Building and maintaining strong supportive connections with business partners, employees, customers, suppliers and the bank.

- *Managing the Numbers*
  Understanding the basic principles of finance and achieving sustainable profitable growth.

- *Marketing, Sales and Customer Service*
  Three essential elements that must be done well to build loyal, long term, profitable customer relationships.

- *Building Business Value*
  Achieving more than simple profitability, but long term business value from the start-up to your exit.

If I can inspire and inform you on these issues, I will have succeeded in helping you to learn from the mistakes of others and avoid making too many of your own.

**"Don't Do It the Hard Way"**

# Contents

Can I help you do better? ........................................ vii
Introduction: Learning Entrepreneurship ................. xiii
Introduction to Uncle Ralph .................................. xvii
Meet the Members of our e2eForum ....................... xxi

1. Welcome to our Meeting ................................... 1
   Why are you here? ..............................................1
   Can you succeed as an Entrepreneur? ......................6
   Don't quit your day job yet ...................................8

2. Starting-Up is Hard to Do ................................. 11
   Initial decisions define the direction ..................... 11
   Choose your partners well ................................... 14

3. Too Entrepreneurial? ...................................... 21
   It's not a good thing ......................................... 21

4. Lead Strategically, Manage Effectively ................. 27
   Start with a plan ............................................. 27
   The Entrepreneur's Challenge:
       Strategic Leadership + Management Effectiveness .. 27
   Keep your head up ........................................... 29

5. Let's do it Again ............................................ 31
   Maybe the first time is your only time ................... 31
   Making money doesn't make you smart .................. 32

6. More than the Bottom Line ............................... 35
   Creating Business Value ..................................... 35
   Being profitable is easy ..................................... 36
   A $600,000 scuba dive? ..................................... 36
   Know your numbers .......................................... 38

## 7. Relationships are the Key .................................................. 41
Employees First ................................................................ 41
Who's squeaking now? ...................................................... 45
Is your Bank a Welcome and Willing Partner in
   your Business? ............................................................. 46

## 8. Marketing is NOT Everything ........................................... 51
It's a Three-Part Process ................................................... 51
Building loyal, long-term, profitable customers ........... 52
Marketing, Sales or Customer Service? ..................... 55
The Six P's of Marketing ..................................................... 56
The Four P's of Salesmanship .......................................... 59
Good Customer Service is Simple, Not Easy .............. 61

## 9. Let's get Personal ........................................................ 65
I am not your mother .......................................................... 65
Business or Family? ........................................................... 67
Listen to Mom ..................................................................... 68

## 10. The Seven Biggest Mistakes and How to Avoid Them  71
The Entrepreneur's Challenge. ........................................ 71
The List ............................................................................... 71
The Answer ........................................................................ 75

## 11. Find the Exit before it's an Emergency ................... 77
From Employee to Owner to Exit .......................... 77
It's worth how much? ......................................................... 78
Pricing your Business ........................................................ 79
Packaged for sale .............................................................. 84

## 12. Wrap-up Roundtable .................................................... 89
What's new with you? ........................................................ 89
What have we done for you lately? ....................... 91

**13. More from Uncle Ralph for Entrepreneurs** ............. **95**
    You have to have a Business Plan – for the
        process, not the product ................................ 95
    Consultants: How to choose, use, and not abuse them 100
    Managing in Difficult Times ................................ 103
    E-Business Challenges for Entrepreneurs ................. 106
    Henry Mintzberg is Worth Listening to ................... 124
    The Best Advice I Ever Got .................................. 126

**Appendices** ....................................................... **129**
    Guiding Principles of the e2eForum ...................... 129
    Discussion Topics for the e2eForum ....................... 135
    Check Lists from the e2eForum ........................... 138
    Recommended Reading List and Some Highlights ....... 143

**Thank you for Sharing** ......................................... **149**
    Entrepreneur to Entrepreneur ............................. 149

**Acknowledgements** ............................................. **151**
**The Author** ..................................................... **153**

# Introduction: Learning Entrepreneurship

*"Don't Do it the Hard Way"*

Entrepreneurs learn to be better and do better in the same way that other people do - they learn from examples and they listen to their peers.

Learning from textbooks can provide an initial understanding of the fundamentals of business and management, but grinding through textbooks is very unappealing to the action-oriented, over-worked and often document-challenged entrepreneur.

We can also learn and be inspired by others - the celebrity entrepreneurs like Steve Jobs, Richard Branson, Mark Zuckerberg, or whoever your star entrepreneur may be. But the lessons learned may not be relevant and their experiences just do not fit the circumstances of most entrepreneurs - those of us who are not yet billionaires and have no corporate jet to visit operations around the world. Maybe it's useful to visualize their success stories as your long-term objectives, but don't get stuck in the day dream.

Let's start with the lessons that are most applicable to your current challenges and opportunities - lessons learned by small business entrepreneurs like you.

In my experience, entrepreneurs get their most valuable input from exchanges with other entrepreneurs. It may be over coffee or lunch, in business meetings, industry associations, networking events, conferences, or formal peer advisory groups like the e2eForum that I describe in this book.

The e2eForum is based on my personal experience with two very successful peer advisory groups that I initiated. The first was the Professional Services Network (PSN), a group of about twelve professional advisors and consultants, including an accountant, lawyer and banker – all senior managers or independent professionals that offered services not products, to businesses not consumers. We had a lot in common and helped each other in many ways – sharing tips and tools, market feedback, strategies and tactics on management, marketing and financing. We occasionally brought in guest speakers to add to the exchange and often worked together on joint projects or promotion of our services. The regular meetings allowed us to extend our networks, knowledge and experience with a group of trusted and competent peers in a confidential, non-competitive environment.

The second initiative was a Strategic Roundtable for entrepreneurs. The approach was to invite a group of my current clients to share their stories, challenges, good and bad experiences and lessons learned. They were all business owners from very different businesses and were surprised to discover how many issues they had in common; like sales management, bank relations, business development or exit strategies. There were no direct competitors, customers or suppliers invited so all the participants were comfortable discussing their failures and concerns, as well as their achievements. Some participants were more open than others and some talked too much. But it was an eye-opening experience for everyone; providing new ideas and generating new confidence in the ability to find solutions.

My objective here is to accomplish the same for you. Please join me, your Uncle Ralph, in an exchange of ideas, information and inspiration with other entrepreneurs in the e2eForum.

After reading the book, you might want to find an e2eForum near you or start one yourself. For more information, please visit: www.e2eforum.com.

To learn more about other elements of entrepreneurship and how to be successful, you may also find it useful to visit: www.LearningEntrepreneurship.com

# Introduction to Uncle Ralph

## *Del Chatterson is your Uncle Ralph*

As you have invested your time and money in this book you have a right to know, "Who is Uncle Ralph and how can he help me and my business?"

So here is my story.

I am your *"Uncle Ralph"*. You can call me Del.

I am an entrepreneur, business consultant, writer, golfer, photographer, happy husband, proud father and grandfather. Originally a small town boy from the Rocky Mountains of Western Canada, I have lived, worked or visited every province and territory in Canada, all fifty states of the US, most of Western Europe, some of Asia and South America. My home for most of the past forty years is the fascinating, multicultural, bilingual, French-Canadian city of Montreal.

I did my MBA at McGill in Montreal, a few years after graduating as an Engineer from UBC in Vancouver.

I have extensive experience in the corporate world, in management consulting and as an entrepreneur with my own businesses. My early corporate experience included financial analysis and systems integration projects, purchasing and materials management with Alcan Aluminum and AES Data. I spent six years with Coopers and Lybrand in management consulting, working with businesses mostly in Canada, but also in Europe and Central America. As an independent business consultant, I have worked with many entrepreneurs, often clients of the Business Development Bank of Canada (BDC).

In recent years, I have gained more international business exposure as a Volunteer Advisor with CESO (Canadian Executive Services Overseas), an agency providing aid to developing economies in Africa, Asia and South America and to Aboriginal communities in Canada. It has been enlightening to share my business ideas and solutions with entrepreneurs in these exceptionally challenging environments of widespread poverty, untrained workers and limited infrastructure. It has provided a very striking affirmation of the extremely favourable economic and political environments where most of us work in North America.

My experience as an entrepreneur and business owner started with TTX Computer Products, an import and distribution business in Montreal. We began with a rough plan and a few estimates of revenue and expense. It was about two years after my last corporate job imploded and I had decided to avoid letting that ever happen again. I wanted to manage my own career plan and started looking for opportunities to start a business while working as an independent consultant. A project in Toronto developing a special educational computer led me to an introduction to TTX and the opening of my own distribution business in Montreal. I was able to grow it from zero in 1986 to a $20 million-a-year business with distribution centres in Montreal and Boston within eight years. And I learned a lot about entrepreneurship.

I then took the business into and out of a corporate merger; for some more difficult lessons in entrepreneurship.

My next start-up venture was with a technology partner in an early e-commerce venture called nxtNet Inc. We got off to a good start, but when the dot-com bubble burst, we wrapped it up like so many other technology businesses and had to come up with a new plan. The learning experience continued.

Over the past fifteen years I have also continued to manage my own consulting business, DirectTech Solutions, working with many different entrepreneurs to help them respond to their challenges and realize their opportunities.

I have assisted entrepreneurs in start-ups and owner-managed businesses in a wide variety of industries at different stages of the business life cycle. The challenges ranged from strategic direction and financial performance to marketing and sales management, cash flow and organisation issues through to planning exit strategies. I have also given courses, lectures and workshops in Entrepreneurship, Finance and Business Planning at both Concordia and McGill universities in Montreal and in other businesses and organizations internationally.

Your Uncle Ralph comes from all of that experience. He is also influenced by my father's good advice and example and by everything I have learned from the many good, and bad, managers that I have worked with over the years. Not entirely coincidentally, Ralph is my secret middle name and was my father's first name. Uncle Ralph is definitely much wiser than I am and has experienced more than I could possibly have lived through myself. He is my alter ego when writing for entrepreneurs.

Uncle Ralph's interest is to share ideas, experience and advice with other entrepreneurs to help improve their businesses and their lives. Of course, I will continue to learn in the process too.

All this knowledge and experience has been incorporated into the writing of this book. My intent is to help entrepreneurs everywhere to learn more and to do better; better for themselves, their families, employees, customers and suppliers; their communities and the planet.

Please enjoy reading the book and sharing the ideas with other entrepreneurs.

Do better.

*Your Uncle Ralph*
Del Chatterson

August 2014

# Meet the Members of our e2eForum

The e2eForum is a group of entrepreneurs sharing ideas, information and inspiration in regular discussion meetings.

The seven e2eForum members that you will meet in the following chapters are:

**Larry** – leaving his day job soon; working on a mobile app for monitoring personal health and fitness.

**Vivian** – a veterinarian and pet store owner, trying to grow her single retail location into a franchised business.

**Brian** – a young entrepreneur in Web development and e-commerce services.

**Stan** – the second generation owner of a small business in heating and ventilation equipment.

**Dave** – an engineer, MBA and former corporate executive, now in import and distribution of high performance bicycles.

**Paul** – age 57, an experienced entrepreneur running a machine shop and thinking about his exit strategy.

… and me, your **Uncle Ralph.**

# 1

## Welcome to our Meeting

*Why are you here?*

"Why do you want to be an entrepreneur in the first place?"

Paul was asking the question because he was getting tired of Larry's rambling complaints: nothing was going as planned; he was not having any fun and still not making any money.

But it was a good question. Most of us ask it of ourselves occasionally and we all have different answers. Larry had probably asked himself the question recently too, but now we were all wondering the same thing.

"If it's that bad, why would you ever quit your day job? Maybe it's time to get back to work on your corporate career."

"Hell no," said Larry. "This business may not always be fun or profitable, but it will always be better than that."

We all agreed.

"Right," said Stan, "I may be a lousy manager, but I'm still the best boss I ever had. It sure beats working for somebody else."

"And it's so satisfying to make your own decisions and live with the results, good or bad," added Vivian.

"OK, so let's talk today about how we got started in business and why we did," I said, "It will help Larry's thinking and give us all a healthy reminder of why we are entrepreneurs. A good start to the day – unless we decide someone made a mistake and shouldn't be here!"

So we adjusted the day's agenda based on the discussion already started. (Not the first time we had done that.)

**Welcome to the e2eForum**

We are a group of entrepreneurs that meet regularly – every third Thursday of the month over breakfast from 7:30 to 9:00AM, missing rush-hour traffic, but before missing any of the work day.

I had started this group about six months ago with **Paul**, the owner of a machine shop who had done well for over twenty years and was now thinking of his retirement plan. We both valued the opportunity to share ideas and experiences with other entrepreneurs, especially in a quiet, confidential environment without any conflicting or competing interests and I had organized similar peer advisory groups in the past.

In the first few weeks, we had added other members and now there were seven of us, including me and Paul. The others all come from different businesses and are at different stages in their business life cycle. You will get to know them better in the next few meetings.

The newest entrepreneur is **Larry,** a young software engineer planning to leave his day job soon to launch a mobile app for monitoring personal health and fitness. He has developed an initial version and is test marketing it with free downloads. He is still drafting his business plan while starting to develop connections with potential strategic partners and sources of financing. He is at the very early-stage of starting his own business.

**Vivian** is a veterinarian and pet store owner. She has run her own pet store and clinic for about six years and is very dedicated to healthy, natural and personalized pet care. She is now trying to develop and expand her single suburban location into a franchised business.

**Brian** is also a young entrepreneur, but has been running a Web development and e-commerce business since leaving university four years ago. He had discovered his aptitude for computer science in high school when he started designing his own computer games. Since then he has learned that he also has an aptitude for business and often impresses us with his ability to manage the technology and the operational requirements of his business while maintaining strategic focus on his long-term plan.

**Stan** is the second generation owner of a small commercial service business. Typical of service businesses, his father started the business as an independent contractor. He was installing heating and air conditioning equipment in residential construction projects and eventually grew his business to eight employees specializing in commercial heating and ventilation equipment. Stan started working with his father after high school and acquired all the necessary industry training and certifications, but struggles with managing the business since his father passed away two years ago and he had to take over.

**Dave** is a forty-something engineer, MBA and former corporate executive, now running an import/distribution business for high performance bicycles. He made the leap when his career plan needed a jolt and his employer offered only more of the same. He was introduced by a fellow cyclist to a new high performance bicycle from Italy that needed marketing and distribution in North America. The opportunity fit with his management experience and it got him excited enough to put in a big chunk of his own money and sign personal guarantees for a line of credit to get started. Now in his third year, he faces challenges to manage both the manufacturer and the bank to keep up with his rapid sales growth.

We were all here this morning and had now agreed on the following agenda.

**Discussion points: How to succeed**

- When to leap?
- What do you need before you start?
- Who will succeed and who will not?
- Why and why not?

All very philosophical questions, but necessary to think about – before, during and after any entrepreneurial adventure.

Larry started with the first question, "So how did you get started as an entrepreneur, Uncle Ralph?"

"Well," I replied, "I often say that starting your own business is a lot like sky-diving – it seems like an exciting idea, but you're not likely to do it until you're pushed out the door."

"In my case, I had literally been pushed out the door of a technology company (AES Data) that was winding down and my number came up. Not a surprise, since I had spent the previous nine months closing facilities and letting people go, but it was a painful experience, nonetheless. I quickly had two other corporate job offers from Nortel and Rolls Royce, both with similar job descriptions and compensation packages, but

I decided it was time to take care of my own career plan and not let someone else decide whether I had a job and what I was doing next. Besides, with an MBA and lots of experience, I was ready to prove that I was at least as good a manager and businessman as the people I had been working for. So I went back to consulting on my own and started to explore opportunities to start in business for myself."

"That's when I met the owners of TTX who were looking for a distributor of their computer peripheral products in Eastern Canada. That appealed to me because it matched my interests in technology and I had good credentials in managing the distribution side of a business. So I quit consulting, put in some cash and agreed to start with no salary as we opened a joint venture in Montreal. It was a great experience from the first day."

As we looked around the table, we realized that we had all arrived at entrepreneurship from different backgrounds and got started at different times in our lives, but we were all attracted for the same reasons.

The attractions that we usually agreed on were:

- Unlimited opportunity to go where you want to go
- Freedom and independence to do things your way
- Continuous challenge and variety of experience
- Responsibility for all facets of the business
- Control over your career and your work/life balance.

However, being an entrepreneur quickly leads you to recognize the less attractive elements of that career choice too:

- There are still limits to what you can do or control
- Many more people are now dependent on you

- The business requires skills and knowledge that you probably do not have
- Your work does not get left at the office
- You now have more at risk and less security in your financial future.

Other entrepreneurs have made some memorable observations that highlight the contradictions:

> *"I used to work for someone that I called boss. Now I work for thirty people who call me boss."*
>
> *"I wanted to be my own boss. But now I have many bosses – my customers, my employees, my suppliers, the bank, the landlord, the government, and the city! It's hard to satisfy them all."*
>
> *"It's still better than working for somebody else."*
>
> *"I'm the best boss I ever had!"*

Which can you say about your business?

**Can you succeed as an Entrepreneur?**

Although you may still be attracted to entrepreneurship, will you succeed? What does it take to be a successful entrepreneur?

It was Vivian who asked, "Is there really an *entrepreneurial type*? What are the personal characteristics, preferences, attitudes and abilities that are essential to success? You've worked with a lot of entrepreneurs, Uncle Ralph, surely you have learned to recognize who will succeed and who will not."

"Sorry, but it's still not obvious to me, or anybody else that I know of. Unfortunately, there is no easy stereotype that applies."

I added, "And if we define success as running a business with continuing profitability and growth, then we also have to admit that success is not always entirely due to the entrepreneur. While I would argue that **_failure is always the fault of bad management; success is not always the result of good management_**."

"Success also requires good luck and good market conditions. Even with good management your business may fail. Not a pleasant prospect, but an important truth. We'll talk about it another day, but my theory is that it's more important to avoid catastrophic failure than it is to chase big success stories. Manage for the small victories that will eventually add up to a big success story. We will discuss it when I present the *Seven Biggest Mistakes that Entrepreneurs Make* and how they can be avoided."

"However, back to Vivian's question, there are some common characteristics of successful entrepreneurs that you can check off for yourself. Here is my short check list of the **Characteristics of a Successful Entrepreneur:**

- Energetic, competitive, independent, confident, persistent, action-oriented, decisive.
- Passionate, persuasive communicator.

If you don't have them all, then you better include a partner in your plans."

"Then before you leap into the unknowns of entrepreneurship, you need to go through another checklist, starting with your *Basic Defensive Interval*."

## Don't quit your day job yet

This time Larry spoke up, "Now I'm getting worried, I haven't got a checklist and I've never even heard of the **Basic Defensive Interval**."

"Not to worry, I had to have it explained to me too the first time I was asked about it. It simply means: *How long can you last without income?*"

"If you quit your day job today, but you still need $3000 a month to live on and you only have $15,000 in the bank, then your Basic Defensive Interval is five months. After that, if your new business cannot afford to pay you at least $3000 a month, then you better have a new day job!"

"OK, so if I need six months to get my business up to speed and I need $5000 a month to live on, then I have to have at least $30,000 in the bank before I quit my day job?"

"Right, but you also have to have enough additional financing beyond the $30,000 for your living expenses to invest in the start-up of your business."

"Got it. If I need another $50,000 in working capital for operating costs, sales and marketing expenses before we generate sufficient revenue to cover them, I now need a cash reserve of $80,000 before launching. That makes it clearer what I need to arrange for financing."

"Now back to the checklist. What else is on the **Before you Launch Checklist**?"

I went to the flipchart and wrote:

- Skills, knowledge, experience, and contacts relevant to your business plan.
- Expectations and preferences for the entrepreneurial lifestyle – work routine and environment, prestige and compensation, work/life balance.
- Personal strengths and weaknesses that will help, not hurt, the business.
- A healthy foundation – family, physical and financial. Solid not shaky.
- Strategic resources in place – partners, suppliers, facilities, key customers and employees.
- Financing for start-up – including your Basic Defensive Interval and the first few months of negative cash flow.

"If you can't put a checkmark with confidence in every box, then you better try harder – recognize the deficiencies and fill in the gaps. Maybe you require more time to develop your skills and get more relevant experience or to beef up your foundation and strategic resources before launching."

"Ouch," said Stan, "Now I know why it has been so hard taking over from my father. I just wasn't ready."

It was time to wind up this e2eForum meeting, but I wasn't sure we had adequately covered the key discussion points yet.

"I think we're good," said Vivian, "I've got to get to work and review the checklist. There are some important elements missing for me too. I will get started now on making the adjustments."

"See you soon everybody. Have a good day!"

# 2

## Starting-Up is Hard to Do

*Initial decisions define the direction*

We were gathered again for our Thursday morning e2eForum meeting and everyone was getting settled.

As usual, Larry was carefully maneuvering his over-laden breakfast plate to the table with a coffee in one hand, plate and utensils in the other and a notebook clamped under his arm. A single guy, it was apparently his best breakfast of the month and he was making the most of it. Others were usually more discrete with a small healthy plate and a large cup of coffee.

Brian was the current chairperson and he was writing on the flipchart:

**Discussion points: Start-up Decisions**

- Strategic Positioning
- Strategic Partnerships
- Business model choices
- Document requirements

As he sat at the head of the table, giving me a wink to confirm that he had used the list I had suggested, he said, "Last month we all found it useful to think back to when we were getting started in business, so I thought we would continue on that theme and discuss some of the other strategic decisions that need to be made in the start-up stage."

Dave interjected wryly, "Maybe we'll discover that we've missed a few. Still it's never too late to get them right."

"Absolutely," I said, "and even if you did make good decisions when you started, your environment will have changed since then and you may need to make new decisions now. At least once a year get out the **road map** that got you started, assuming you have one, **called a Business Plan.** Check whether you still have the same destination and that you're still happy with the route you chose, the bus you built and the passengers you're traveling with."

"OK," said Larry between mouthfuls, "the rest of you are far enough along to look back and do that review, but I'm just getting started. What are the first key business decisions to make?"

Since he was at the very early stage of business start-up, I gave him the same suggestion I give to new entrepreneurs in my Business Planning class. "Start by coming up with a name and a marketing slogan. That will define how you want to be seen by your customers compared to all the competing alternatives they have."

"Defining yourself relative to the market is called **Strategic Positioning** and it's a very important early decision. Do you want to be seen as the IBM of your industry - competent business professionals, or more like Disney - fun and friendly? Will your corporate image be that of prestige and performance like Porsche or rugged utility like Jeep? This is an early requirement soon after you have defined the business opportunity and chosen your business model - the decision on your strategic positioning and how you wish to be perceived by customers."

"Your choice of strategic positioning will only be realized if it is consistently communicated and demonstrated. It should influence *everything* in your business – from office décor and business cards to your website design, sales rep's dress code and automobile choices, customer service policies, product pricing and packaging. It is the starting point in defining your corporate culture."

Paul was the first to respond, "I have to admit that we arrived at our positioning and corporate culture by default, not by design. My history in machine shops gave me the experience and confidence to trust my instincts. I just did what seemed right to me whenever I had to make a decision. And now it's too late to change the stripes on this old tiger."

"Not an unusual approach, Paul," I replied. "Most entrepreneurs go by instinct and personal preference on these questions of strategy and corporate image. Consequently, the corporate personality is often very much a reflection of the owner's personality and style. Which is fine; if they are appropriate to the business and attractive to its prospective customers. If not, then the corporate image can probably still be presented favourably enough to attract business. Where it is more likely to be a big problem is when the owner's contradictory management style is applied inside the organisation and corporate culture to the point that it has a negative effect on attracting and managing quality employees."

There were some quiet nods around the table as they thought of their own familiar examples and my mind wandered back to my own worst experience.

## Choose your partners well

After eight successful years of rapid growth and good profitability in computer products distribution, I had decided to expand and grow to the next level by entering into a merger with a new business partner. *What a disaster that turned out to be.*

Strategically, it made great sense – complementary product lines, expansion into more territories, a more balanced portfolio of customers and suppliers and great synergies in sales, marketing and administration. But what I saw from the outside was not the same personality that was hidden inside my new partner's business. From the outside, it appeared to be a successful distribution business with high-value specialty products and good quality customers. I had known the owner for many years and we had done some business together in the past. He was charming, knowledgeable and had succeeded with some good product lines. But, as I often said afterwards, it was like knowing somebody well at the office, then suddenly discovering when you go into his home that he kicks the dog and yells at his kids.

After the merger, I was exposed to his completely dysfunctional management style. Abusive, selfish, and paranoid with his employees; they feared him, never gave him any bad news and imitated his aggressive style among themselves. It was surprising that they had survived at all and it soon ended badly for the merger. A true personality conflict – both for the two companies and the two owners. Let's just say, 'We no longer do lunch.'

"Which leads us to the next important point," I said, coming out of my mental detour, "choosing good strategic partners."

"But I'm never going to have a partner," said Stan, "One thing my father insisted on – you can rely on your family, but never bring in a partner."

"But you already have **strategic partners**," I said, "Your key managers and your banker, your biggest customer and the major suppliers that you depend on. You need to make good choices on them all. I didn't always and most of us have suffered the consequences of choosing some bad partners."

"So in spite of what your father said, let's talk about business partners that might be more valuable to your business than the available family members, maybe even more trustworthy."

"Oh man, have I got some stories for you," added Paul, "about a brother-in-law and a nephew I wish I'd never met. We don't have time this morning for me to tell you the whole story of how my wife insisted that they could help my business; then they almost put me out of business. Believe me, they are not allowed anywhere close to my shop anymore."

"No family in your exit strategy?" asked Dave.

"Only if I can adopt a bright, capable entrepreneur like you or Vivian," replied Paul. "Too bad you're both already occupied."

There were a few other grumbles around the table as conversations continued about bad experiences with family members getting involved in the business.

"Dealing with family members, though, is a good place to start setting the ground rules for everyone directly involved in your business," I suggested. *"It is essential for every business to clearly define the roles and expectations of the owners as __managers__ separately from their rights and obligations as*

<u>shareholders</u>. Don't even start the business without signed shareholder agreements and key employee contracts."

"In the area of legal agreements and financial structure, you should seek professional advice from lawyers and accountants before making the classic entrepreneur's mistake of neglecting the formal paperwork. Small omissions in these technicalities can get very expensive when the unexpected actually happens."

"It would be inappropriate for me to give you advice in those areas, but I do have a checklist you can use to cover all the essentials."

"Oh good," said Larry as he pulled his notebook out from under his empty plate, "another checklist."

I smiled at him and flipped over the discussion points for today to start a new sheet, headed *The Start-up Document Checklist*, commenting on each point as I wrote:

1. Business Plan.
   "Often neglected, always necessary. And I wrote the book, as you know. For anyone who needs a copy of my *Do-It-Yourself Guide to Business Plans*, I always have one in my briefcase. I won't do the whole speech today, but you absolutely have to have a documented business and financial plan for start-up, to manage the business and to prepare for exit." (Actually, that is pretty much the whole speech.)

2. Shareholder agreement.
   "Include all the standard terms, but ensure you understand the buy/sell provisions, especially the 'shotgun' clause. You want to have a prior arrangement for any partner to buy in, buy more or sell out."

3. Life insurance on each other.
   "You don't want to suddenly have a dead partner then find yourself working with the husband or wife as your new partner. Life insurance allows you to buy out your deceased partner's interest and avoid that conclusion."

4. Incorporation.
   "There are other business structures, such as a sole proprietorship or a partnership, but I always recommend incorporation to prove that you are serious about your business and have provided a structure to build upon. Especially if you plan for your business to be more than a temporary, part-time job."

5. Business licenses and regulatory approvals.
   "You'll be surprised how many regulations there are, whatever business you're in. And ignorance is no defense when the auditors and inspectors arrive. Do your homework and pay the fees; it's always cheaper than paying the penalties later."

6. Information systems.
   "Start by making good choices on your information systems. The essentials are an accounting, invoicing and management information system; office productivity tools for preparing documents, quotes and proposals; and a contact database system or customer relationship management software for business development and customer service. These can amount to large initial investments on start-up, but if you decide to avoid them and start small, be sure that there is an upgrade path to support your growth to a world class business. You don't intend to stay small do you, Larry? " He had no comment, just a self-satisfied smile.

7. Leases and contracts for facilities and services.
"Here you can make your own list depending on what you need for your particular business."

"OK," I concluded, "these are the essential documents for start-up. Now did everybody here do them all before they launched and announced to the world that they were in business?"

"Off course not," said Paul, as he looked around the table, "We all started knocking on doors before we had incorporated, written a business plan or had a supplier contract. Learn by doing, right Dave? Vivian?"

Even Brian was nodding sheepishly, as if it was an admission he was not as organized and cautious an entrepreneur as we all thought.

"That's my experience too," I admitted, "It usually takes a year into the business before you complete the checklist. But I'm sticking to the list as a minimum requirement for good management of your business."

Stan was starting to pack up for the office and left us with his action item for the day, "We've been in business for twenty-seven years and we're long overdue for *the Start-up Document Checklist*. It's on my To-Do List now."

"Me too," said Paul, "maybe a little late, but it will still help me put together everything I need before I launch my exit plan."

"The document list is good," said Brian, "but I am more concerned about reviewing our strategic positioning. We have some notable inconsistencies in presenting our corporate image between the 'technology experts' and the 'helpful service providers' so I'm going to look at our marketing campaigns and website to make it clearer that we are both competent and user friendly."

Stan added, "Yes, I also made some notes about our current strategic partners and we need to do some re-alignment there too."

"Sounds good," I said, "Lots to follow-up on at the next meeting. See you then."

# 3

## Too Entrepreneurial?

*It's not a good thing*

Brian was still chairing at the next meeting, but he had a look of concern; unusual for him as he was normally upbeat and confident.

Gesturing to the flipchart, he said, "These are the issues that are starting to wear me down. Mostly because my two senior managers in sales and project management are starting to tell me I'm not entrepreneurial enough."

We looked at his list.

**Discussion Points: Too Entrepreneurial**

- Opportunistic
- Optimistic
- Impatient
- Confident
- Decisive
- Creative

He added, "Uncle Ralph, when we were working together on my original business plan, you warned me about the risks of being too entrepreneurial. These are the points I remember and I thought we could discuss them today in the e2eForum."

"But they all look good to me," said Stan, "my father was always pushing me to be that kind of entrepreneur."

"It all comes down to balance," I said, "Balancing the entrepreneurial instincts and drive with the well thought-out strategic planning and analysis that help you make good decisions."

"Let's go through the list," said Vivian, keeping us on the agenda.

I opened by explaining my perception that although certain characteristics of entrepreneurs are necessary for them to be successful; too entrepreneurial can be a problem for the business.

I went over the points that I had previously discussed with Brian while we worked on his business plan and he was bubbling with entrepreneurial enthusiasm. My intent was not to dampen his energy and enthusiasm, but to provide some perspective on the risks.

**Too opportunistic.**

It can be hard to resist every potential sale or customer opportunity that is presented to you, but the successful entrepreneur builds the business by remaining focused on the strategic objectives and the agreed action plan to get there. Time and resources are easily wasted on chasing rainbows, if you are not sufficiently selective and insistent on sticking to the plan.

Both current customers and new prospects will continuously presented unexpected opportunities. If they are asking for it, you should do it, right? Well, maybe not. Can you do it well? Profitably? Better than the available alternatives?

Your Go/No-Go decision should be based on two strategic requirements: leveraging your competitive strengths and building long term business value. Those are the two selection criteria that will keep you focused.

**Too optimistic.**

It is important to be optimistic and think positively, but a little paranoia may be wise too. Remember the chairman of Intel, Andy Grove, titled his memoir *Only the Paranoid Survive.* Mark Zuckerberg has been credited with the same mentality in driving the astonishing growth of Facebook. Keep a wary eye on the market and monitor your business performance constantly. No news is not good news; you're flying blindfolded. Don't miss or ignore the warning signs of bumpy weather approaching.

**Too impatient.**

Don't expect too much too soon. It seems like everything takes longer than it should and most entrepreneurs have high expectations of themselves and their team. But don't keep changing the plan or trying something new just because you're not there yet. If you are making progress and the end goal is still valid, don't give up too soon.

**Too confident.**

Entrepreneurs usually have great confidence in their instincts and their intelligence. The mistake is to neglect or ignore market feedback and analysis of the facts. Also being action-oriented, the tendency is to react and 'fire' before the 'ready, aim' stages are complete. Painful surprises can result. Temper your self-confidence with a little humility – ask for help and get the input from others before you rush ahead.

**Too decisive.**

Entrepreneurs are expected to be decisive and demonstrate leadership. But both can be overdone - deciding too quickly and providing too much direction so that employee input, initiative and creativity are stifled.

Often the decision does not need to be made quickly and the implementation will go more smoothly if time is taken to assess the feedback and answer the questions before commitments are made and the wheels are put in motion.

Back in the `80`s, Japanese management style was the model of success and one of their recognized tactics was to talk and talk and talk about the solution before implementing it. The result was much smoother and faster implementation than for the stereotypical macho decisive American manager who decides quickly and starts implementation without sufficient prior consultation with those affected.

**Too creative.**

Many entrepreneurs are driven to 'Do it my way'; that's why they love running their own business. But sometimes alternatives have not even been considered and a better way exists. The creative solution may require improvising and learning on the fly, but maybe the best solution is sticking with what works, until it stops working.

Another mistake is staying too long with a solution and neglecting to evolve and grow by optimizing systems and processes and installing the best practices and latest technologies available in the industry. Not everything needs a creative new solution unique to your business. Maybe you're not that special.

I summarized for the group, "Those were the points I had discussed with Brian and my assessment of the risks of being too entrepreneurial; all these mistakes can lead to serious difficulties for the business."

Dave added, "It does help to keep in mind that some careful analysis and planning are important to offset the tendency to make decisions based on instinct and past experience. I've had to make some quick decisions recently that I'm now going back to re-think."

"See you all in a month and we can talk about what changes we have made to avoid being *too entrepreneurial*."

# 4

## Lead Strategically, Manage Effectively

*Start with a plan*

As we started our e2eForum on a bright sunny spring morning, this was on the flipchart:

*The Entrepreneur's Challenge:*
*Strategic Leadership + Management Effectiveness*

It is my favourite theme and I had been asked to decide on today's discussion topic, so there it was. Some around the table had heard me rant on this subject before, so I was trying to approach it a little differently.

"Today I'm going to start by admitting to you my own biggest mistake as an entrepreneur – failing to continually think strategically. I was too often pre-occupied with operating issues and short-term problem solving. Stuck in the old dilemma of too busy fighting fires to ever work on fire prevention."

"This was especially true in my first business, computer products distribution. There was so much detail to keep on top of – markets and technologies, customer service issues, managing employees and learning everything I had to know as a new entrepreneur about running a business – from accounting systems and freight rates to lines of credit and payroll deductions."

"I had all the usual excuses for being drawn into the daily crises and never getting back to the drawing board to review the original strategic plan and see if we were still on track. To be honest, our original plan was not very strategic and never looked past the first two or three years. It was only focused on making our numbers, not on strategic positioning and managing our important business relationships. We made good short-term decisions to maintain profitability and win our share of competitive battles, but did not effectively protect ourselves from conflicts with our major suppliers and were not prepared for the rapid decline in profit margins as competitors flooded the market."

"We started our business in the mid '80's when IBM personal computers and the clones and compatibles were first landing on desktops everywhere – in offices, schools and homes. With our one primary product, computer monitors, we were initially competing with only about six major brand names and maybe four other regional distributors."

"Our customers were mainly the local computer stores that were on every second street corner and in every shopping centre. We were selling a few hundred monitors a month and average profit margins were at 12% to 14%; pretty healthy we thought. But high profits and fast growth brought a lot of competitors into the market. By the mid '90's we had over forty competing brand names and at least twenty competing distributors. Profit margins in distribution slid to about 4% - no longer healthy. Our volume was up to ten times over our second or third year, but net profit was the same and we now had huge risks in inventory and receivables."

"That's when I made the decision to enter into the merger which would have helped us to diversify our product mix and customer portfolio and reduce the risks. Unfortunately, the merger didn't work and I subsequently left the computer hardware industry two years later. Very quickly after that consolidation eliminated most of the players in personal computers – only a few major brand names, three large multinational distributors and three or four national retail chains remained by the year 2000."

"Any of the survivors from that era had to be very good at re-positioning their businesses to keep up with the rapid evolution of the computer business."

"Your own business may not see rapid change like the computer industry, but I'm sure that whatever business you are in technology and the Internet continuously affect how you do business. You have to adapt to keep up with changing competition and new customer expectations."

"Don't make the mistake I did of getting lost in the operating details and neglecting to raise the periscope and scan the horizon for oncoming threats or opportunities. Be prepared to respond."

*Keep your head up*

"I do try to keep aware of what's on the horizon," said Dave, "but sometimes I have very limited choices available for my response. We expect our manufacturers to keep up with the technology and the competition and our bike dealers to do a good job of attracting customers and making the sale. As the national distributor we provide the pipeline to market, but we need the people at both ends to work with us."

"And it is true," he added, "even if we're in 'old economy' traditional businesses, we all have to keep up with technology – both to remain competitive and to rise to new customer expectations. The devices and applications all keep getting cheaper, easier to use and more effective at delivering the results. We simply cannot afford to stand still – the competition will beat us and the customers will leave us if we don't keep sharpening our tools."

Looking around the table it seemed we all agreed with Dave. Strategic vision and leadership need to be constantly applied to daily decision making.

Lack of strategic direction, in my opinion, may be the biggest mistake for entrepreneurs and can be fatal to the business.

# 5

## Let's do it Again

*Maybe the first time is your only time*

We all tried hard to arrive early for the e2eForum meetings because it gave us time to chat informally with the other members and exchange comments on our businesses and other issues that were not on the day's agenda.

Unfortunately, an accident on the expressway this morning had kept me from arriving early enough to review the agenda with Stan, who was chairing the meeting this week.

The discussion had already started and this was on the flipchart.

**Discussion points: Serial Entrepreneurship**

- Another Start-up?
- Or the next Screw-up?

What I heard was, "It looks like a safe investment and my son has some experience in the restaurant business. I've got the initial $60,000 and bank financing is easy because they love franchises." Paul was talking about the gourmet hamburger franchise he was considering investing in.

"Sorry, Paul," said Dave, "but experience flipping burgers doesn't mean your son knows how to run a burger joint. Even if the franchisor delivers all the management tools and support, do you really want to manage minimum wage staff and deal with unhappy customers complaining that your burgers suck? Your experience is all about managing highly qualified machinists and selling precision parts to multinational manufacturing businesses."

"Yes, but I built a successful business in that industry, so this should be much easier. I have the time and the money and I need a new challenge to keep me interested. I don't want to spend every day in retirement watching my money ride the stock market roller coaster."

"It sounds like your entrepreneurial juices are percolating, Paul," I said, "Maybe you should go back to the start-up criteria we talked about a few months ago. Look for an opportunity that really leverages your unique skills, knowledge, experience and contacts. Isn't that what worked for you the first time?"

"True enough. All I bring to this business is a long history of eating hamburgers!" Dave was laughing at himself and it looked like he would leave his money in the bank – for now.

I was remembering what I have said to other successful businessmen:

### Making money doesn't make you smart

What I said out loud was, "Before you throw your energy and money into a new venture, ask yourself a few important questions."

"I hear another checklist coming!" chirped Larry.

"Thanks Larry, now I'll have to give it a name."

"Let's call it the **Encore Performance Checklist**. If you are determined to boast that you are a serial entrepreneur, not just a successful entrepreneur; then ask yourself these questions before you get started on your next venture:

- What was it that made you succeed in your first business? Did you build your business on your unique management ability, a new product idea, a preferred customer or supplier relationship? Which of these will apply to the new business?
- What mistakes have you avoided in the past? Are you about to make them now? What new risks are you encountering for the first time?
- Is now a good time to start something new? Are there no challenges left in your current business?
- How much will a new initiative impact your current business and the demands on your time and resources?
- Is your past success really transferable to a new business?"

"Many successful entrepreneurs have made the mistake of jumping into a new venture - merger, acquisition, restaurant franchise or real estate investment - and blown away the equity value they built in their original business. It's another costly mistake to avoid."

Brian shared his conclusion with us, "I'm now convinced that the next venture is something to set aside until I'm at the exit stage like Paul. When my current business is running itself and I have the time and money to *very carefully* select the next opportunity. I just don't want to wait until I'm that old, sorry Paul. I'm thinking I'll be ready for the next one at age 35."

Stan added, "Too late for me, I'm already 39, but I'd like to accelerate the plan to get to that stage soon too. Then I can start the next one before I get bored and screw up the one I've got."

I said, "I have seen that happen. Entrepreneurs who started to dabble in something more exciting, thinking their business was on cruise control and it headed into a crash landing instead."

"So let's avoid the unhappy ending of exit by default. Put it on the agenda for a future meeting – *Preparing for Exit.*"

We all agreed that was a good topic for a future meeting and concluded the e2eForum with our regular Roundtable update from each of the members before heading out for the day. (*See Chapter 12.*)

# 6

## More than the Bottom Line

*Creating Business Value*

Most entrepreneurs get into business because they are good at something and want to do more of it, but on their own. Then they discover there are two basic management subjects that they are not good at – Financial Management and Marketing.

This meeting of the e2eForum was going to be focused on Financial Management and I had suggested the following discussion points.

**Discussion points: Financial Challenges**

- Profit versus Long-term Value
- Managing the Balance Sheet

"Let's start with the same question that I ask my students in the first class on Financial Management: 'What is the primary purpose of every business?'"

"Make a profit!"

"Thanks Larry, I was counting on you for the wrong answer. Go sit in the corner. Sorry, but I needed that answer to make my point that the real purpose of every business is **to create long-term shareholder value**."

Vivian interjected, "But isn't that just another stereotypical response by big business defending their obscene profits that is being so strongly criticised by today's socially responsible consumers and shareholders?" She looked agitated and added, "Please don't tell us *Greed is good!*"

### Being profitable is easy

"No, I'm not going to defend the excesses of unregulated capitalism or socially irresponsible companies. I believe very strongly that modern, enlightened capitalists and entrepreneurs will do best for themselves and their companies, their employees, their customers and suppliers, their communities, society at large and the planet itself; ***if they focus on building long-term shareholder value.*** The right decisions will flow from that focus."

"And a focus on short-term profits will do exactly the opposite. It is easy to improve short-term profit by reducing the maintenance and marketing expenses, neglecting product development, cutting employee wages and benefits, ignoring safety and environmental regulations and avoiding taxes, but these actions can all destroy long-term value. Paying attention to these requirements will help to build it."

### A $600,000 scuba dive?

"We're talking about financial management, but short-term sales management decisions can also lead to value-destroying results. Taking the low margin, high credit-risk order just to meet the sales revenue target can be very bad for your business."

"Let me tell you about my own experience with a very scary scuba diving trip. And it wasn't because of the stingrays."

"My daughter started scuba diving while she was at Queen's University and had learned to dive in dirty, cold Lake Ontario. Then she persuaded me to get certified so we could dive together on a one week trip to the Cayman Islands in the warm clear waters of the Caribbean. It was spectacular diving on a fascinating variety of coral reef. We were having a great time with two or three dives a day off remote Cayman Brac. There was only one phone line back to the office, but I was confident that all was well in the capable hands of my management team."

Then one afternoon walking through the hotel lobby, I heard, "Mr. Chatterson, we have a fax for you."

It was a handwritten note from our technical services manager, *Del, we have a problem with about 400 monitors in the federal government. The last shipment seems to be off-spec and our dealer Antares, is refusing to pay. They owe us $600,000.* It was suddenly not a good day at the beach."

"After a long sleepless night, I decided to call the senior partner at Antares and take an aggressive tone accusing him of abusing my staff and threatening to ruin my business. He quickly backed off and said, 'No, no, no. We just weren't sure how to reach you and wanted to get your attention. We can look after it when you're back.'"

"Which we did."

"But I got a lot more careful about managing my receivables risk. A few years later when Antares did go into bankruptcy, we lost about $24,000. Bad, but not enough to kill my business. That scary scuba trip was a sharp warning to start managing credit risk better while growing fast."

## Know your numbers

"Speaking of financial management, most entrepreneurs are very focused on managing their bottom line by monitoring sales, gross margin and expenses. They always know those numbers, right Dave?"

"Yes," Dave said, "but in distribution it's easy. I know the sales results every day; track profit margins by product line and can tell when I have covered my monthly fixed costs."

"That's good, but do you know the industry benchmarks for the key performance variables, beyond average gross margins? What about sales per sales rep, revenue per square foot of warehouse space or freight cost as a percent of sales, average inventory turnover, working capital ratios and average days in receivables or payables?"

"Jeez, now you're picking on me!?"

"No Dave, I know you are better informed and manage the numbers better than most. But we all need to keep our eye on the scoreboard and track our results by monitoring the key performance measures against the benchmarks for top performers in our industry and against our own history to be sure we are staying on track and correcting any variances by continuously making improvements."

"The caution I have for you, is that most business owners neglect asset management, especially cash flow. The business may appear very profitable, but actually has constant cash flow challenges because management is neglecting inventory and receivables, in particular. Unfortunately it is not as simple as the old rule of retailers: *Collect fast, Pay slow*. Both customer and supplier relationships can be at risk if cash flow issues force you to be too aggressive in collections and too lackadaisical in payments."

"Managing the balance sheet also requires good management of your bank financing to balance the short-term and long-term needs with short-term and long-term types of loans. Working with your banker is a very important element of good financial management."

"Let's talk more about that at our next meeting. I'll see you then."

As I rushed out to my morning appointment, I noticed a few pained expressions in the group as they were mentally running through their own accounts receivable issues.

# 7

## Relationships are the Key

*Employees First*

This was on the flipchart:

**Discussion points: Key Relationships**

- Employees before customers
- Biggest before loudest
- Bankers as partners

Stan was leading the group today and started with, "OK, let's start the discussion with a question. Which relationship is the most important key to success for any business?"

"Customers, of course." And it wasn't just Larry with the obvious answer this time.

"OK, then which relationship can be the biggest obstacle to your success."
"The bank"
"Employees"
"The government with all their regulations and reporting requirements"
"Suppliers, who don't deliver as promised."

Now we had some differences of opinion. So I interjected, "Can we all agree though, that we cannot keep our customers happy and coming back for more if our employees don't treat them well? And the best way to ensure that happens is to treat our employees the way we would like them to treat our customers."

"Isn't it always obvious to the customer when the flight attendant, service technician or waitress is not happy with her job?"

"The best lesson I ever got was in Las Vegas (and it's a story that should not stay in Vegas). We were at the annual computer conference and exhibition there (COMDEX) and my partners and I were having a long breakfast meeting in the Treasure Island Casino dining room. Long after breakfast we were still getting smiling and prompt service from the waiter with never-ending cups of coffee. We were there for so long that the shift changed, but we still had friendly, attentive service from the waitress who now was bringing the refills. Finally, after we had remarked on the service among ourselves, I said to her, 'We have been coming to this conference in Vegas for many years and have met in many different dining rooms, but this is absolutely the best service we've ever had. How do you do it?'"

"She said, 'The owner, Steve Wynn, treats us so well, we treat everybody well in return.' Boom. She got it and the message stuck for me."

"Great story, Uncle Ralph, and I agree," said Brian, "but what if that well treated employee just doesn't get it."

"That happens. I remember a service technician telling me that his sharing in the monthly sales bonus made no difference to him; he still treated all the customers like idiots. Apparently we had made a hiring decision that was a mistake; so we asked him to leave and take his attitude elsewhere."

"Recognizing and removing the misfits is a difficult but necessary part of people management. If employees do not buy into the corporate culture they will never be effective members of the team and need to be removed. Doing it well is important because all of your employees are watching and judging you as a manager."

"When I was doing a survey to develop my list of the 'The Seven Biggest Mistakes that Entrepreneurs Make', one entrepreneur suggested it should include *"Hiring too Fast, Firing too Slow."* He had a good point and it reminded me of the time I made both mistakes with the same employee! (More lessons learned.) And I know you want to hear that story, right?"

"Sure," said Larry, "I find it reassuring to know you made so many mistakes and still survived!"

"Well, let's just remember the old cliché, 'What doesn't kill you makes you stronger.' Or as Bill Gates used to say at Microsoft, "in this business you have to recognize your mistakes quickly, before they get big enough to kill you.' Most of the time I did fail fast and move on, but my merger was a big mistake and it did kill my business because I didn't reverse the decision fast enough. Fortunately, I 'survived' because I had a good network of business associates, employees and customers, as well as enough cash on the side, to re-start. That's something else you need to do. Make sure you can survive the failure of your business by taking out enough cash for yourself and your family. Build that *Basic Defensive Interval* again for next time."

"But back to Bernie (not his real name, of course), and my mistake of hiring him too fast and firing him too slow. He was a sales rep with a bit of a mixed track record and some contradictory references - 'great guy, good results, but hard to manage'. Of course, I thought I was a better manager than his previous bosses and I needed a sales rep, so signed him up. He did well for a few months, bringing some new customers with him and getting some big orders for us. But he was hard to keep track of and I started to notice his work habits were letting us down. Late for meetings or not showing up at all; refusing to make the extra effort if it interfered with his 'personal' time."

"So after about a year, one more refusal to go out of his way for a customer caused me to sit him down and *'counsel him out'*. (That was the clumsy euphemism we used to use at Coopers and Lybrand to advise someone that their career plan would be better served somewhere else. Instead of delivering the very clear message, 'You're fired!') Then I compounded my errors by trying to be kind and giving him some good referrals to other companies that might be hiring. That wasn't doing him or his next employer any favours.

Immediately after he had left us, I started to learn from employees and customers that he was an even bigger problem than I thought; not only were his working relationships contentious with everyone, but he also had another business on the side that he was working at with his wife when he was supposed to be working for us. 'What took you so long to let him go?' was the common theme."

"So in terms of hiring, firing and managing performance, I learned to include other managers in the process and to be much more observant of who are the team players and who are not. Who get it and who do not. To recognize good or bad performance and to encourage feedback my guiding principle remains: *"Praise in public; Punish in private,"* but it is never quite that simple."

"Dealing with poor performance is only one of the challenges in managing employee relationships."

"Recognizing and rewarding high performance employees is also a very important priority, even if they need less supervision and micro-management. They need to be engaged and developed to meet their own goals. You need them to act as if they are owners too – always working to promote the company and improve its performance. Mismanaging high performers puts at risk the most important resource required to build value in your business."

### Who's squeaking now?

"Back to the all important customer relationship," said Vivian, "the same principles apply to managing good and bad customers. I find it's easy to make the mistake of being distracted by the most annoying and persistent customers and neglecting the biggest and best customers who are not likely the 'squeakiest'; just the most important. They are easy to forget because they require less service, but it's a big mistake to neglect them. Not only do they bring important revenue to the business, they also influence a lot of other customers. They deserve VIP treatment."

"Right, Vivian," suggested Dave, "But don't forget to also squeak more yourself. Do your suppliers appreciate you enough? Maybe you are more important to them than you realize. For example, you may discover that they love you for always paying so promptly and you can get preferential pricing or terms, if you just ask. I know it can make a big difference if you push your suppliers to do better for you."

He added, "My most important supplier is actually my bank and they are just not keeping up with my rapid sales growth."

"We started with a line of credit of $50,000 at RBC bank, supported by personal guarantees and secured by our inventory and our receivables with the bike shops. But sales are growing so fast the bank is calling it 'over-trading,' which means they are not comfortable with the rapid increases that have brought the credit limit up to $750,000. They will not go to $1,000,000 in spite of the good history and the solid security, because according to the credit manager 'we are at the limit for consumer products in our branch portfolio.' That is not helping me, so I'm going to BMO who have been aggressively seeking our business and they like our financials. They are willing to give me everything I want – higher credit limit, lower interest rate, reduced personal guarantees and a few other goodies like better foreign exchange rates and electronic funds transfers. I'm signing next week. Believe me; it pays to build and maintain a good banking relationship."

I had to give credit to Dave for a very instructive story as I started to hand-out the article I had planned to circulate today. "Thanks Dave, that's a good introduction for me to leave you all with this article on banking that I wrote for my Blog a few years ago."

### *Is your Bank a Welcome and Willing Partner in your Business?*

> Many business owners do not consider their bankers as welcome and willing partners in their business.
>
> Yet it is an important relationship that will often affect your ability to grow and to survive periods of financial stress. You want to treat your banker like your best customer, not your worst supplier.
>
> Working with an unwilling and unwelcome partner is obviously not a very constructive relationship. A more effective partnership with your banker can be built on some of the following assumptions:

**1. They will not get it.**

Start by accepting that your bankers will never fully understand what you do for a living - your motivation, your challenges or your circumstances. But you do have to try to get them to understand enough about you and your business operations so that they can be confident that working with you will be good for them.

Remember the bank's primary role is <u>not</u> to lend you money; it's to earn a return on their investment for their shareholders and limit the risk of losing any money.

**2. It's only for the money.**

You will need to prove that the money is all you need; because you have looked after everything else.

The banker does not want to worry about your customers, your management team, your sales and marketing efforts, your operating efficiencies, your health, your marriage or anything else except the financial services you need.

**3. They have a checklist.**

When you meet and fill in the forms, remember the banker wants to be satisfied on these five criteria:

- **Character** – do you have a reputation of integrity and responsibility on prior financial obligations?
- **Capital** – do you have enough invested in your business to be personally at risk?
- **Capacity** – do you have good potential to support the cash flow requirements?
- **Collateral** – if you cannot repay your loans, what assets are available to cover them?
- **Conditions** – is your industry in good economic condition or in a downturn?

Good answers on these points will provide the start to a good relationship with a confident and willing partner instead of tentative support from a cautious and reluctant partner.

### 4. Reduce the risk.

You may be stimulated by risk and reward; your banker is not. Banking is a very conservative career choice. Regardless of how good you and your plans are, the banker will still want personal guarantees. That means he gets your house if you fail. (Note: I have never met a banker who found it amusing to suggest that you should get <u>his</u> house if you succeed.)

### 5. Think big.

The more you need, the more interested they'll be and you'll likely get better terms. (The only time I had no personal guarantees was when our loans were at $4.8 million.) So, if you're starting small, be sure to describe your growth plans and your intention to build a strong, long-term banking relationship.

### 6. Get a second opinion.

Bankers love to win business away from other banks. That's good for their career plans. (That's how we got the $4.8 million with favourable terms.) So check out the competition anytime you need new financing or your current bank is not serving you well.

Just be sincere and be ready to change. One banker asked me directly, "If I meet all your requests will you move to my bank?" I said, "Yes". Then he delivered and so did we.

### 7. It's not a people business.

It's a numbers business and you cannot negotiate with a computer. That friendly, helpful person you're talking to does not make the decisions. Your numbers get fed into some obscure computer program and the answers (or more questions) pop out. They are not negotiable. A good banking relationship means that you will be told what numbers are required to get favourable answers.

### 8. Manage your numbers

Make sure your business plan computes and gives financial results that are attractive to lenders. Then manage the numbers to deliver the results and stay within the limits set by the bank. Read the fine print to be sure you don't miss any requirements to maintain financial ratios or any restrictions on payments to shareholders. Deliver financial reports as required, but also be sure to provide your own analysis and explanations before someone else does. You don't want that computer to set off the alarms.

### 9. No surprises, please.

Bad news is never well received, but the reaction will be much worse if it's also a surprise. And no news at all only makes them worry.

Keep your banker aware of what might go wrong and what you plan to do about it. Then keep them current as things evolve so they get used to your ever-changing circumstances and how you are handling them. (Hopefully, well.) Avoid going back with a new plan too soon or too often. And try to plan well ahead of any request for more financing. It is very hard to get the bank to help you out of a disaster when you're in it.

### 10. People still matter.

The personal connection is still a very important part of a good relationship with your bank. Part of managing that relationship is to be sure that you are not entirely dependent on just one contact. If the relationship lasts, your contact person will change and you need to know someone else to maintain continuity of the relationship. Stay connected at several levels.

Your banking relationship needs to be strong to withstand the inevitable hard times that hit any business. A welcome and willing partner should help you weather those occasional storms.

It was an old article, but it still seemed to strike a chord as everyone slipped it into their notebooks, exchanging their own stories of unsupportive bankers as they left the meeting.

# 8

## Marketing is NOT Everything

*It's a Three-Part Process*

Today's discussion was being led by Dave, who considered marketing to be his biggest strength and the key to his rapid success. He started with, "Marketing *is not everything*. But it is the first important step in a three-part process to deliver satisfied customers who keep coming back for more."

"So these are my key points for discussion today."

**Discussion points: Building your Business**

- Goal = Long-term, loyal, profitable customers.
- Process = Marketing + Sales + Customer Service

"Who wants to start?"

"Let me add," I said, "that marketing is an area that entrepreneurs often either neglect or do badly. Kind of like the restaurant business; we're all exposed to it enough that we think we understand how it works."

"OK, OK. I've given up on the hamburger business," said Paul with a laugh.

"Glad we helped you avoid that misadventure", I said, "But I want to emphasize Dave's two key points on the goal and the process.

*Building loyal, long-term, profitable customers*

> **Goal:** All efforts must be dedicated to the primary objective of every business: building loyal, long-term, profitable customer relationships
>
> **Process:** It's a three-part process of Marketing + Sales + Customer Service.

It's all about finding, attracting and retaining customers that bring value to the business in continuous profitable revenue and also become our biggest fans, telling everybody how wonderful we are. Sometimes we get so preoccupied with the hard work managing our marketing and sales efforts that we forget that essential strategic objective."

"The financial objective, of course, is to generate and grow sales revenue and profits. But to have sales you need customers. And to have sustained, profitable and growing sales, the best strategy is to develop loyal, long-term customer relationships."

"So the marketing, sales and customer service activities must all be aligned to deliver a customer experience with your company and your brand that evolves from a first time buyer to a long-term customer. The marketing and sales efforts bring in the first order and then customer service has to deliver on the rest."

"The **customer experience** with any business should evolve through four levels:

1. **Satisfaction with price and availability**
   On the first exposure to your business, customers will quickly, maybe even subconsciously, compare price and availability to their expectations derived from prior experience with your competition. If this minimum expectation is not met, there will likely be no sale and maybe no second chance.

2. **Recognition of superior service levels**
   The first point of differentiation and the first step to building a stronger customer relationship will be when the customer recognizes that you offer superior service. You can demonstrate it in many ways – more stock, better delivery, easier payment terms, faster response to inquiries or better warranty service and support. Any one of these may be sufficient for you to stand out from the competition and deliver a satisfied customer.

3. **Appreciation of the value of your knowledge and experience**
   After the basic needs of price and availability are met and you have distinguished yourself with superior service, the customer experience should then lead to an appreciation of the added value of your knowledge and experience. This will be demonstrated by your staff having the product knowledge, training, education and experience to help customers make better purchasing decisions. Now you are building a relationship valued by the customer.

4. **Connection on values, mission and vision**
   The final step in cementing loyal, long-term relationships will occur when the customer recognizes a common sense of values, mission and vision in the way you both do business. This connection will be developed over

several interactions, particularly when problems are solved together, or you connect on issues not directly related to the buy-sell transaction like honesty and integrity, social values or environmental issues."

"The sooner you can meet customer expectations at all four levels, the faster you will build lasting and loyal customer relationships. And that is the primary objective of every business, right? Does anybody think 'buy once and goodbye forever' is a business model that works for anybody?

Vivian had an answer, "Well, if you're selling kitchen appliances, it might be ten or fifteen years before the customer needs another one."

"Also true for high performance bikes," said Dave, "they may make only one big purchase every six or seven years. And that's why bike shops try to add accessories to their product line – helmets, shoes and clothing – as well as keep in touch with the customers for service and tune-ups. Most have a Website and Blog or Twitter account or an e-newsletter to build brand loyalty through the levels 3 and 4 that Uncle Ralph mentioned – demonstrating the added-value of their knowledge and experience as well as confirming common values and vision around biking."

"I recognize that we do that in our combination of pet store and vet clinic," said Vivian, "It's all very complementary services and products 'sharing the love' for peoples' pets. We already have customers that have lasted longer than their pet!

Brian raised his hand to interrupt, "These are all good concepts, but what about all the little things we need to do? I have a technology business that is immersed in the digital side of business and all our marketing, sales and customer support services are done online with Web marketing and e-commerce applications, but I think some of the traditional principles still apply."

"You're right Brian, the key elements still apply," I agreed.

*Marketing, Sales or Customer Service?*

**Are choices to be made? Do we need to deliver on all three?**

"First let's define better the three elements of this process to build long-term valuable customer relationships:

1. **Marketing** – understanding the market and defining the target customer; building awareness, interest, and attraction; and identifying prospects.
2. **Sales** – converting interested prospects into qualified, buying customers.
3. **Customer service** – delivering products and services as promised to ensure that each customer is a satisfied, repeat customer."

"Each step has to be done consistently well for the results to be achieved. But a choice still has to be made - which element are you going to do best? Will you win from competitors on marketing, sales, or customer service? You cannot be *best* at all three."

"In my experience managing a second-tier brand name in computer hardware, we knew that we couldn't possibly out-market the multinationals, but we could out-sell them – one customer at a time. We spent a minimum of time and effort on marketing. Respecting basic principles of clear and consistent messaging and being creative at avoiding large expenditures worked for us. Winning on customer service was also a challenge - it's expensive for any manufacturer to compete on warranty terms and technical support. So we went back to salesmanship, even in the service department - coaching staff on persuading the customer to be reasonable, patient, and give us another order, please! We carefully explained to our service technicians that the best result from a call for tech support was to turn a complaint into a compliment and then pass the call to a sales rep for another order."

"You can achieve success by being selective, instead of trying to be good at everything. So take a look at your strategic positioning, your performance and your options in marketing, sales and customer service - then choose, focus and build one of them into your competitive weapon."

### The Six P's of Marketing

"Now Brian, you did ask for a checklist and I just happen to have one prepared for today," I said as I passed copies around the table. "You've probably heard of the Marketing "Four P's", well I have re-organized them into six. No extra charge."

"You need to build your marketing objectives and plan around these six P's: three strategic and three operational. Here's the checklist."

> STRATEGIC:
> 1. **Positioning:**
>    - Strategic positioning of the product relative to competitors in the target market sector will affect all the other elements – placement, promotion, product, pricing, and packaging.
>    - Choice of high versus low in quality, price, and service.

2. **Placement:**
   - Where is the product or service to be made available for customers?
   - Choices of retail or wholesale, online or storefront, direct sale or through distributors and sales agents.

3. **Promotion:**
   - Choices of priorities, budget and effort.
   - Direct marketing, advertising.
   - Public relations activities, participation in industry associations, conferences, trade shows,
   - Website, search engine optimisation and web marketing programs.
   - Promotional items, sponsorships.

**OPERATIONAL:**

4. **Product:**
   - Description of the product or service.
   - Features and benefits offered relative to the competitors.
   - Product development plans to meet changing market demand.

5. **Pricing:**
   - Determined by the market, target market sector, competitors and customer expectations.
   - Market price relative to cost is the primary determinant of profitability for the business.
   - Volume discounts, incentives, or variable pricing?

6. **Packaging:**
   - Choices of style, colours and packaging consistent with the corporate image, identity.
   - Warranty, service, accessories, literature, included?

- Meeting regulatory requirements?
- Retail display, shipping & handling issues?

"And that's pretty much the one page course in Marketing, which is all we have time for today, since we haven't talked about sales management yet."

"How do we know if that's a problem?" asked Larry.

"It's always a problem," said Paul.

"Only if you neglect it," said Dave.

And I added, "You know there is a problem brewing when you hear an entrepreneur explaining that 'The product sells itself', or 'Price is all that matters', or 'Our Sales Reps need to do a better job'."

"These complaints are signs the company is failing at both marketing and sales management. Not only are opportunities for profitable growth being missed, but the company may be on the downward slide to 'out of business' without a well-conceived and sustained marketing plan and effective sales management."

I went over to the flipchart, "Here is my approach to Sales Management."

### Guiding Principles of Sales Management

- o **Sales objective** is to make targeted prospects into active customers.
- o **Sales process** is to take leads from marketing, qualify them as interested prospects, make the sales pitch and get the order.

- o **Sales rep** needs to be known, liked, respected and trusted, *in that order* for sales success.
- o **Remind the rep**: Sell yourself first, then the company, then the product.

"It is, of course more difficult and complicated than that, but for basic Sales Management, these guiding principles will get you a long way."

*The Four P's of Salesmanship*
**Patient, Persistent, Polite and Persuasive**

"OK, now I have to tell my favourite story on salesmanship. Not an original and probably not even true, but very instructive anyway." They looked a little concerned, but I continued.

"A high-powered IBM executive working in New York used to take the subway to the office everyday and he noticed there was a young man always positioned at the top of the stairs to the street with a box of books at his feet and two or three in his hands, politely asking every passerby, "You wanna buy a book?" He was there rain or shine, hot or cold, every morning and evening as hundreds of commuters passed by. After several months of observing this hard-working, polite but persistent, casually dressed, but personable young man asking everyone who passed, "You wanna buy as book?" the IBM executive stopped one morning to speak to him."

"He said, 'Young man, I am very impressed with you working so hard here everyday and I would like to offer you a job at IBM. We can get you started in our sales training program and within a year or two you could be making $60,000 to $80,000 a year.'"

"The young man politely replied, 'Why thank you very much, sir, but I'm already doing better than that. You wanna buy a book?'"

Dave laughed out loud as others smiled and he said, "I'm definitely telling that story to one of my reps who is trying too hard and making it too complicated. He's reading books, going to courses, sitting in on Webinars, following the experts on Blogs and so on, but he gets so caught up in the process that he neglects to just ask the question, 'You wanna buy some bikes?'. It drives me crazy sometimes listening to him on long distance to Vancouver or San Francisco ramble on about the weather and the football and the economy before he finally asks about their inventory and gets to the point, 'Do you need some bikes?' In fact I'm putting this on the agenda for our next sales meeting: *Keep it simple and ask for the order.*"

That got such a good response I couldn't resist another sales story. I started with a short preamble.

"A suggestion I often have for sales managers is to recognize their top sales reps and get them involved in sharing their tactics with the other reps. Learn from the best. It's also a good way to build the sales team by sharing ideas and information, like we do here. If it doesn't go well, it may be a warning sign that your sales compensation plan is promoting competition and jealousy instead of co-operation and teamwork."

"So I have another story to help you remember that principle of sales management. (I probably should give credit to the great Zig Ziglar for these stories. But I honestly don't remember where I heard them first; I've just been repeating them for years.)"

"This story is about a company selling safety glass that had a direct sales force calling on customers all over the U.S. Each year they had a sales conference where they celebrated their successes and recognized the top achievers. For several years, old Charlie had won the top sales award, so one year they asked him what he did to win so many orders. He was willing to share and explained, 'When I finally get an appointment, I sit down with the buyer and I bring out the samples of our safety glass to compare to the samples of our competitors. "Then I bring out my hammer. And I smash them all right there on the conference table! Now I have their attention to make my pitch.' Well that year a lot of sales reps went out with their samples and their hammers."

"But again Charlie won the top sales award."

"So again the VP of Sales asked Charlie, 'What did you do this year?'"

"Charlie said, "I gave the hammer to the buyer.'"

"OK, enough checklists and bad stories to take away. Now just remember the secret formula: *'Sell like hell!'* Never quit selling. Get your team focused on the one thing that solves all your problems – more sales."

### Good Customer Service is Simple, Not Easy

"Now we've talked about getting the customer's attention through effective marketing and getting the order through good salesmanship, but what about the final step to deliver a satisfied repeat customer – exceptional customer service?"

There were a few sheepish looks around the table, but Vivian spoke up, "I think that's what we do best. We suck at marketing and sales, because we're all so respectful of the customer that we are reluctant to appear at all pushy. Our style is very much in line with our whole approach to the business –*How can we help you take better care of your pet?"*

"Sounds exactly right," said Dave, "Your staff are immediately aligned with the customer on the top level of vision and values. You can probably still work on the marketing to get people into the store and salesmanship to get the staff to push for sales, but you are already doing well at attracting and retaining loyal customers."

"I agree," added Brian, "it's the best way to close a sale; demonstrate your interest in the customer's problem before you present your solution. Listen before selling. Remember the old consulting mantra: 'They don't care what you know until they know that you care.' It works for us."

I added, "I've noticed though that when entrepreneurs are trying to understand their customer's needs, they often mistakenly assume that they think like a typical customer. But that is not always the case. It may be true for Vivian as a conscientious pet owner, but most of us have to do market research and customer surveys to keep up with our customers' changing needs and expectations and listen carefully to what they say."

"Not always easy to do, as the customer is not always right and seldom reasonable. But it is a good simple rule. Listen to what the customer wants and then find a way to deliver it. As customers ourselves, the last thing we want to hear is, *'I'm sorry but company policy doesn't let us do that'....*"

"Maybe the first rule for customer service is to make sure everyone knows how far they can go in breaking the rules. We all love to hear that customer service rep in the Philippines tell us that she can fix our billing problem and also reduce our contract fees by $12 a month. A simple gesture that removes the sting of getting ripped off for the previous six months."

"The important point about customer service is the one that we made earlier talking about key relationships. ***Employees need to be treated well if we expect them to treat the customers well.***"

We had covered a lot of ground on marketing, sales and customer service (not to mention too many anecdotes), and we were well past the regular 9:00AM deadline. So we agreed to postpone the Members' Roundtable and wrap it up for this meeting of the e2eForum.

I heard Stan mumbling to himself on the way out, "So much to do better, so little time in a day." It is another frequent challenge for entrepreneurs: applying what they learn and making the changes required, while managing the daily demands on their time.

# 9

## Let's get Personal

*I am not your mother*

Today we had agreed to talk about personal issues that affect the business, particularly issues involving the family in the business.

This was on the flipchart:

> **Discussion points: Personal Issues**
> - Family in or out?
> - Employees like family?

Paul started the discussion by reminding us, "I've had some bad experience with relatives interfering with my business, but mixing family and business isn't all bad. My wife has been a tremendous help at critical times over the years and both my son and daughter pitched in during the early years to do some of the grunt work. It was good for them, too. Exposed them to business from the inside and probably helped persuade them to head for university and get into a good profession, instead of running a business like me!"

"For me it was different," said Stan, "I started working summers with my Dad, then after high school I thought I wanted to do something else, so went to work with a big construction company. That's when I realized I was happier to be in a small, more personal business and returned to work with my Dad. I appreciated the satisfaction and the recognition that comes with being close to management and clearly contributing to the success of the business."

"And that pretty much sums up the challenges," I said, "How do you include family members that are interested and still give employees who are not part of the family the same level of satisfaction. Can you make them feel they are accepted as an effective part of the team without getting too involved in their personal lives? How do you treat them well without confusing the boundaries between boss and employee? How can you be friendly without being friends?"

Dave said, "That was about the first lesson I learned as a young engineer after getting promoted to production supervisor. Within a week or so I had to suspend a friend for three days without pay for a safety violation; in spite of the fact that I had spent the weekend water-skiing with him. It was tough to remain friends after that."

"It is a choice of management style," I said, "I've seen it all – from 'use and abuse them' managers to the paternalistic godfather who insists on getting involved in all his employees personal lives."

"The first is dysfunctional because it requires micro-management of every detail and creates an 'us-versus-them' work environment. But the paternalistic style goes too far in the other direction, I think. It creates a sense of dependency, relieves employees of their sense of responsibility and reduces their willingness to take initiative and make decisions. My preference is a management style that is respectful and kind, but encourages employees to think and act like part-owners of the business. Encouraging a sense of responsibility and a willingness to make decisions and take initiative, even if it means accepting mistakes and their consequences. That style also makes it easier to manage the business and to eventually exit as the business becomes much less dependent on the owner/entrepreneur."

### Distracted by Personal Issues

"Unfortunately, you can still be distracted by personalities and personal issues that may seriously affect business performance. The distracting personality may be an owner, manager or employee and it can be a mistake if the issues are simply ignored until they become a problem."

"The problems may be a clash of personalities affecting working relationships and they have to be dealt with one-by-one by the supervisor. Sometimes these problems come from the top performers that get carried away and start behaving like rock stars."

### Business or Family?

"Family businesses have particular issues to navigate," added Dave, "My kids too, worked in the business during the summers and it was a challenge for them and me. My daughter was very uncomfortable as the boss's daughter, but my son managed to fit in and even started calling me Dave at work, instead of Dad. Maybe that was the secret."

I said, "Yes, family members in the business add some new challenges. On the other hand, as Stan's father told him, family members can usually be trusted to take a greater interest than outsiders in the business. Sometimes, however, that can be a problem too. I was invited at one time to help manage a business where the owner's daughter was the office manager. Unfortunately, she was protective of his interests to the point of being paranoid and obsessive about every detail. She was so aggressive and tactless about it that we actually hired one receptionist who quit before noon the first day because of her. I eventually persuaded the owner that both his business and his daughter would benefit if she made her career plans elsewhere."

"Even if your family is not in the business, they can still have a powerful influence. I don't know about you, but I'm still trying to impress my mother and follow the advice of my father."

**Listen to Mom**

"Yeah, that never ends," said Stan, "even after they're gone."

"My mother once told me, 'Don't do anything you wouldn't do if I were there.' That got my attention and was a great way to keep me on the straight and narrow as a teenager, but I still imagine her checking up on me every day."

"Worth keeping in mind as entrepreneurs," I said. "Mothers are an important influence to guide our ethical conduct in business too. I like the way it was stated by a jeweler in Cranbrook BC who had a conspicuous sign posted next to the cash register stating 'We give instant credit to all our customers. If they are over 90 and accompanied by their mother.' Great credit guideline!"

"Most entrepreneurs and executives probably don't often think of their mothers on the job – unless she's the boss, like Ma Boyle at Columbia Sportswear. Maybe they should. We would probably have fewer issues of CEO misconduct, if their mothers knew what was going on. Perhaps instead of all those business management courses and books on ethics and corporate responsibility, we only need to remind decision-makers to ask themselves "Would my mother be proud of me if she knew what I was doing?"

"And as your Uncle Ralph, I'm still inspired by my father's unique character, style and wise advice, reinforced with easily remembered one-liners, like 'Always do good work but charge like Hell!' He had enough like that to fill my next book!"

"But my mother also had a strong influence on my management style, although she was more subtle. It was less frequently stated than demonstrated. Quiet, hard working, good humoured, responsible and respectful of others; those are the characteristics that immediately come to mind. Things we all learned from her example, simply by being around her. Of course, she was also good at reminding us when we forgot those important principles or our behaviour was not up to her standards. And it's still a pleasure to make her proud. That's why I recommend you use the test 'What would Mom think?' before taking action and making decisions in your business."

**But I am not your mother**

"Now I'm suggesting that we might have better decision-making if we asked ourselves what Mom would think. But what about those employees that expect you to act like their mother?"

"What is the right level of caring and compassion before it becomes more personal than a working relationship should be? Is there a reasonable limit? Is it appropriate to get involved with issues that are strictly personal? Do employees become part of your extended family with all the additional obligations that that implies?"

"Some recent exposure to business owners dealing with their employees' personal issues has caused me to be more cautious about getting involved. Once managers start offering a sympathetic ear and then a shoulder to cry on, it soon becomes more time consuming on and off the job and creates a relationship that is difficult to steer back to business only. It also becomes a distraction for other employees and creates new concerns about employee favouritism."

"My guideline for these situations would be to decide whether you would or should do what is being requested for every employee in the same situation. Offer financial advice or a cash advance? Special working hours or more time off? Bring the baby to work? If not, then say no to the first request. Don't start a precedent that you're not prepared to offer to everyone and write into your corporate policy manual. (You do have one, right?)"

"And don't be afraid to clarify the relationship, 'I'm your boss, not your mother. This is a business not a social safety net.' Not cruel, but kind. And in everyone's best interest."

The meeting came to a close and there were a few quiet reflective moments as we all thought about the role of family in our businesses.

# 10

## The Seven Biggest Mistakes and How to Avoid Them

*The Entrepreneur's Challenge.*

In the preceding chapters we have worked our way through what I call *the Entrepreneur's Challenge.*

Once you have your business started, the real challenge will be to successfully keep it growing and profitable. There will be many opportunities to make mistakes and to stumble into unexpected problems.

From my experience, confirmed by most entrepreneurs, it is normal and acceptable to make mistakes as long as they are small and recognized early. You will fail occasionally. It's all part of the learning experience to get better.

But there are some big mistakes that can kill your business.

*The List*

This is my list of the *Seven Biggest Mistakes that Entrepreneurs Make.* You will notice that we have covered all seven through discussions in the e2eForum.

### #1 Too Entrepreneurial

Certain characteristics of entrepreneurs are necessary for them to be successful. But if over-indulged they can lead to big mistakes. These include the tendency to be too opportunistic and not sufficiently selective and focused; to be too optimistic and miss or ignore the warning signs; to be too impatient and expect too much too soon.

Entrepreneurs usually have great confidence in their instincts, but the mistake is to neglect or ignore market feedback and analysis of the facts. Being action-oriented, the tendency is to "just do it".

Entrepreneurs are expected to be decisive and demonstrate leadership, but both can be overdone – deciding too quickly and providing too much direction so that input, initiative and creativity are stifled.

All these mistakes can arise from being "too entrepreneurial".

## #2 Lack of Strategic Direction

Another tendency of many entrepreneurs is to get lost in the daily details and completely forget their original strategic plan. Operating decisions demand continuous attention and there is seldom time dedicated to stepping back and looking at the business from a strategic perspective. The common observation is that the owner is too busy working *in* his business to effectively work *on* his business.

Defaulting to continuous short-term decision-making can result in the business not having consistent strategic direction and straying far from the original plan.

Lack of strategic direction may be the single Biggest Mistake that Entrepreneurs Make.

## #3 "That was Easy, Let's Do It Again!"

Another common mistake that can have devastating consequences on the business is the over-confident entrepreneur who concludes, "That was easy, let's do it again!" So he or she jumps into new markets, new product lines, or even a new business or investment opportunity without doing the homework first.

It's important to remember: Making money doesn't make you smart.

It is important to look at every opportunity with the same detached analysis as the first time you started a business.

Many successful entrepreneurs have made the mistake of jumping into a new venture – merger, acquisition, restaurant franchise or real estate investment – and blown away the equity value they generated in their original business.

Another big mistake to avoid.

## #4 Focused on Profit

Being focused on profit doesn't seem like a mistake. After all, isn't that the whole purpose of running a business? No, actually. As we discussed, the primary financial objective of any business is "to enhance long-term shareholder value."

Many short-term profit-oriented decisions can hurt long-term value. Most entrepreneurs are very focused on managing the bottom line by monitoring sales, gross margin and expenses. They always know those numbers. But they are often neglecting asset management, especially cash flow.

Managers need to look at all their key performance variables and react quickly to avoid big mistakes.

## #5 Neglecting Key Relationships

The key relationship for any business is the one between management and staff. Good communications are essential to providing strategic leadership and ensuring that management and staff are working effectively as a team toward common goals.

Sometimes we are distracted from our key relationships by the most annoying and challenging employee or customer. Often your biggest customers are not the "squeakiest" just the most important. And do you need to squeak more yourself? Do your suppliers appreciate you enough?

Another important relationship is with your banker: Is your bank a welcome and willing partner in your business?

Building and protecting these key relationships are essential to keeping your business on track and meeting your strategic objectives.

## #6 Poor Marketing and Sales Management

There are usually obvious signs of poor marketing and sales management. Feedback from customers will also highlight your failures in customer service. Opportunities for growth are being missed and current customers are fading away.

No business can survive without effective marketing and sales management supported by consistent customer service. All three functions need to be done well to build loyal, long-term profitable customer relationships.

## #7 Distracted by Personal Issues

Personal issues can seriously affect business performance regardless of whether they come from the owner, management or staff. Family businesses introduce particular challenges to managing personalities and corporate culture. Can you include family members in the management team without excluding others?

In summary, my list of the **Seven Biggest Mistakes that Entrepreneurs Make**:

1. Too Entrepreneurial
2. Lack of Strategic Direction
3. "Let's do it again!"
4. Focus on Profit
5. Neglecting Key Relationships
6. Poor Marketing and Sales Management
7. Personal Distractions

*How to Avoid Them?*

*The Answer*

Each of these Big Mistakes is a result of the entrepreneur failing to achieve balance between opposing forces.

*The Answer is Balance!*

Avoiding these mistakes requires the entrepreneur and business owner to:

- Balance Energy and Drive with Planning and Analysis
- Balance Strategic Vision with Operational Detail
- Balance the Logical Head with the Intuitive Heart

- Balance Short-term Profit with Long-term Value
- Balance Personal Priorities with Strategic Objectives.

Balance these issues to grow and prosper in your business and avoid the *Seven Biggest Mistakes that Entrepreneurs Make.*

# 11

## Find the Exit before it's an Emergency

### *From Employee to Owner to Exit*

Dave was running this meeting of the e2eForum, but we were all looking at Paul, who had just been asked by Vivian, "You are the closest to retiring from your business, Paul. What stage are you at in planning your exit strategy?"

"Thanks for reminding everyone I'm the designated 'Old-Timer' in the group," replied Paul with a twinkle in his eye confirming that he was still a young entrepreneur at heart, "I don't have much progress to report, only a lot of ideas and questions rattling around in my head. That's why I'm starting on the *process* with the really old and very wise Uncle Ralph"

"Thanks for that introduction," I said, "I'm not sure whether to deny the 'really old' or 'very wise' or both! How about I just share my version of the *process* you described and you can all decide for yourselves which is true. I have written the key points on the flipchart."

"But that just confirms what an old-timer you are!" Larry was chirping again from the end of the table. "We really should introduce you to the modern world of PowerPoint."

"We've been introduced, thanks Larry. I will dazzle you another time with PowerPoint. I'll even give you some great tips on how to do better than your last one. Or you can look up Guy Kawasaki's 10/20/30 Rule for PowerPoint yourself. (It's a simple rule: 10 slides, 20 minutes, 30 point font). Don't look so offended. Your presentation was OK, just not great."

"Anyway, in these meetings I prefer to keep it simple, informal and avoid the frustrating challenges of *technical difficulties*. Felt pen and flipchart are pretty reliable, as you can see."

"Does this cover the questions you have, Paul?"

### Discussion points: Preparing for exit
- Establishing business value
- Enhancing business value
- Management succession plan
- Exit strategies

"Yes, let's get into it before someone suggests I also need to learn PowerPoint."

So I started, "OK, the first steps are establishing and improving business value which, as we've already discussed, should be done continuously from the day you start in business, but valuation comes up most often at the exit stage. Then it's no longer an academic question, it's more 'What price can I get for my business?' And unfortunately, there is no right answer until somebody actually signs a cheque. If you'll allow me, here's another brief story to give you an idea of what I mean."

### *It's worth how much?*

"A former client with a well-established technology consulting business in Montreal called me back a few years ago to give him my assessment of the value of his business. So I did my homework. He had over twenty years of consistent profitability, a good reputation in the industry, some proprietary software products and major international corporate accounts. All that helped enhance the valuation and led me to estimate a price of $3 million to $3.5 million for his business."

"He agreed that seemed reasonable, then said, 'But I already sold it for $6 million.'"

"What?"

"So he explained that he had accepted an offer from a big European competitor in the same industry that wanted to acquire his business and had offered him $6 million. However, he then discovered that once they owned it, they planned to shut it down and move the operations into their office in Philadelphia."

"That's when he said 'No thanks', at any price. But he did proceed with a plan to sell equity to his key employees based on an agreed value of $4 million. All to demonstrate that the value always depends on the intentions of the buyer and the seller and what they want to achieve by the transaction."

"However, even understanding that in advance there are still some basic principles to establishing a price for your business."

I proceeded with my presentation on pricing and packaging your business.

## Pricing your Business

I usually recommend that a simple estimate of the value be included with the financial projections in every Business Plan. The principles of valuation are well known and the math is quite simple. But the real price is established only when a particular buyer and seller actually agree and sign on a price and terms suitable to their current circumstances and objectives, as illustrated by this story.

If you are managing as an owner-entrepreneur then you should always be focused on maximizing the value of your business. That means understanding what determines the price. Not your ego-inflated value of the business, but the price that a dispassionate investor or buyer would put on it.

In establishing the value of your business, some basic principles must be recognized:

1. The value to the owner is unique to that individual. Ego may artificially inflate the price, but more importantly the value is often very dependent on the current roles and relationships established by the owner and may change drastically with his or her departure, thereby reducing the price offered by a new prospective owner.

2. Value is always determined by an evaluation of the future income relative to the uncertainty or risks associated with achieving it.

    Regardless of the valuation method, the forecast future income stream has to be credible and the potential risks have to be reduced to get the best possible valuation.

3. Current owners tolerate more risk, uncertainty and fuzzy circumstances than new owners or investors. You may be OK with the fact that you are dependent on one key supplier because he is an old buddy from high school; or that you have no signed lease because the landlord is your favourite uncle; or that your best sales rep is also your daughter and she wants to be president.

Prospective buyers will be much less enthusiastic about these issues, unless they are all resolved to their satisfaction in advance of any offer to purchase or invest.

4. Different buyers will accept different prices, terms and conditions.

   Those usually range from the passive investor looking for a reasonable return with reasonable risk; to the active investor who sees the potential to do better than your forecast under his own management; to the strategic investor who sees even greater opportunity in buying a competitor, supplier or customer and merging it with his existing business to increase revenues, eliminate unnecessary overheads, and substantially increase profits.

   The selling price will depend on the perceived value seen by each of these buyers.

Several valuation methodologies may be used and it is often a good idea to test different approaches to see what values they yield and then select a selling price that can be reasonably supported by any method of valuation.

## P/E Multiple

The price-to-earnings multiple is a well recognized valuation method and is widely reported for public companies. Current price per share divided by annual earnings per share is a simple concept and easily calculated. Unfortunately, it is not always very relevant, since the selling price today is more likely based on the expectation of future earnings, not last years' earnings. The same may apply to a valuation of your business.

For example, Google's share price on January 15th, 2014 was $1150 which yields a P/E multiple of 26X based on 2013 earnings of $44.19 per share. But, if we use the analysts' consensus earnings estimate for 2016 of $71.74 per share then the P/E multiple is a more "reasonable" 16X. Still high compared to the less exciting Royal Bank of Canada priced at $70.90 per share with a P/E multiple of only 10.3X earnings for 2016.

What is the P/E multiple for your company?

Typically, small owner-managed businesses can support a P/E multiple ranging from 3X to 5X. It will be higher if future earnings are very secure and not dependent on the current owner and lower if future earnings are risky and very dependent on the current owner.

The buyer will usually look at operating income or EBITDA (Earnings before Interest, Taxes, Depreciation and Amortization) to determine profitability of the business, before considering financing, taxes and capital costs. For example, that will yield a price of $300,000 on your $100,000 per year operating income, if you can agree on a P/E multiple of 3X and a price of $500,000 if you can persuade the buyer that a multiple of 5X is reasonable.

**Payback Period**

Some buyers will insist on looking only at net cash flow and the payback period to arrive at a price. They will consider their net investment, after allowing for financing, taxes, incentives and payment terms to determine how long before they get their investment back and start earning positive cash flow. They will likely have a minimum payback period, depending on risk, ranging from 3 to 5 years (which yields essentially the same price as a 3X to 5X multiple of EBITDA).

## Discounted Cash Flow

Other investors will take the financial analysts approach of calculating discounted Net Present Value (NPV) or the Return on Investment (ROI). Again the future net cash flows must be forecast to arrive at a valuation. The buyer will then discount future cash flow at the required rate of return on the investment, typically 15% to 20%, or calculate the expected ROI and then compare it to the required rate of return. For example, a $100,000 per year annual cash flow on a $500,000 investment provides a 20% annual Return on Investment.

Using these same methods will give you a range of valuations depending on various buyer/seller scenarios to establish your own best estimate of a fair selling price.

Now you have a methodology for determining the value of your business over time. It will be useful for getting initial investors and will also help in any shareholder buy-sell agreement or succession plan.

Knowing the value of your business is a key performance measure that you should be tracking regularly. The day you need to know it should not be the first time you calculate it. Don't wait until your exit is an urgent necessity; always have a price and a plan.

As I concluded and watched the e2eForum members taking notes, I waited for the next question which usually followed.

Stan was the first to look up and ask it. "I just did a quick calculation and I don't like the answer. So how do I improve on the price for my business?"

"You are all probably doing the first two things that enhance business value; growing sustainable profitable revenue and reducing business risk. The next important priority is management transition. How do you evolve from employee to owner to exit? It is very hard to get a new owner to buy your business if that buyer cannot replace you and your value as manager in the business. If you can transition yourself from active manager to passive investor or 'absentee owner', it will then be much easier to transfer ownership."

## Packaged for sale

I continued, "Even if your business is not for sale, you should be planning to make it less dependent on you anyway. Otherwise you are self-employed, but not yet an entrepreneur who owns a business. And true entrepreneurs always manage their business to maximize its value – for themselves and for future owners."

"It may *not* be a short-term objective to exit your business, but it is always a healthy management strategy to package your business as if it's for sale."

"That means making it independent of you, the owner, and ensuring that the performance metrics are attractive and easily understood by outsiders. Meeting those two criteria will immediately make the business more valuable and also less demanding on you, until you are ready to exit."

"It essentially means looking at your business as a dispassionate investor, instead of the emotionally committed owner. Step back and look at your business as it would appear to an outsider, who is trying to put a value on it."

Remember that business value is based on only two things:

1. the expected future income and
2. the degree of certainty or risk associated with it.

The issues that affect forecast future income and the business valuation multiple are:

- Strategy, competitive positioning and branding
- Product or service plans, pricing and quality
- Cost control – both variable and fixed costs
- Asset management - cash, inventory, receivables, facilities and equipment

Performance tracking and improvement efforts will require analysis of the financial ratios compared to your industry, specific competitors if possible, and checking trends over time. A future buyer, not to mention any banker or potential investor, will consider all of these factors.

The issues that affect risk in the business are:

- Reliability of financial statements
- Dependence on a few major customers or suppliers
- Dependence on key employees, especially the owner or family members
- Quality of management, employee relations
- Customer and supplier contractual relationships
- Competitive threats
- Condition of facilities and equipment
- Financial obligations, loans, leases
- Protection of products, intellectual property, trademarks, brand names, exclusive territories
- Potential liabilities – product failures, warranty claims, product recalls
- Regulatory issues – taxes, legal, environmental, social

After presenting these points, I added, "You can enhance the value of your business simply by working on increasing the returns and reducing these risks. That usually means making the business more profitable, more stable and less dependent on you. It probably means installing a management team that can deliver the results without your direct involvement. That is always worthwhile because it will be easier for you to exit at some point in the future and reduce the demands on your time in the short term."

"*Packaging your business for sale* helps you immediately to make it a better business; both more valuable and easier to manage."

Dave spoke up first, "More good checklists and a strong reminder to focus on transition to managers that can ultimately handle the whole business. Otherwise we'll never be able to exit and cash out."

"Yes," said Vivian, "and a reminder to keep working on the strategic plan away from the preoccupation with daily details. I'm seeing more clearly that if I don't install a capable manager in my store and another vet in the clinic, I'll never develop the packaged business model that I need to move forward with franchising."

"I found that was the first step in growing my business beyond being a self-employed Web designer and programmer," said Brian, "When I hired someone to do the projects, I could then focus on project management and business development. Now I have managers in those two functions and seven programmer-developers doing what I used to do. The next step is to make myself completely redundant, but I cannot yet afford to hire someone as general manager and I'm not sure whether either of the two current managers can move up to that role."

*Find the Exit before it's an Emergency*

"Those challenges are all part of the process," I said, "I currently have three clients working on their exit strategies, not including Paul. One business has a hard-working husband and wife team that has done well over many years. Now they would like to retire, but they have been profitable by keeping lean and have filled all the senior management roles themselves. So they have no one in place for transition of management and it is very difficult to find a buyer for the business who is able to invest in it and then work as hard as they have."

"Another client looking for the exit has a strong well-qualified management team, but none of those managers are interested in assuming the risks and responsibilities of becoming owners, so the only option is to transition to absentee owner and he is not yet confident enough in his team to do that."

"The third client has a small consulting business that is very much tied to his own professional skill and personal client relationships. Already in his late 60's, he is still responsible for managing the business and selling the work. In this case, we are working on a merger or acquisition partner that could integrate the clients and consultants into their business and allow the owner to transfer responsibilities to their senior management team and ease himself out. We are still working on the match-making."

"All three should have planned for their exit before they got to this stage."

Stan spoke up, "It would be nice to have my business go to the third generation in the family, but my kids have already said they don't want to join me in the business, so I have to look harder at management transition in my retirement plan too."

We started to pack up for the day back at the office, but our heads were all in the distant future and thinking about two important questions.

How will I exit?

What will my business be worth?

# 12

## Wrap-up Roundtable

Before ending the meeting, it was time for our usual e2eForum Roundtable; each member providing an update on their business and sharing any other news.

***What's new with you?***

Larry started, "Thanks to Dave for spending time with me on my business plan, it really helped to have the feedback. Of course I used Uncle Ralph's *The Complete do-It-Yourself Guide to Business Plans*, but doing it yourself is still not easy. I am continuing to test market the product with free downloads and that is helping me with both product development and the business plan. I should be ready to launch in three to four months."

Vivian was next, "My big news is that I now have a new partner and investor in the franchise concept."

Polite applause and, "Congrats", "Way to go Vivian!" from the other members.

"Thanks," she said, "She's a long-time customer who has become a friend and is really interested in helping us grow through the franchise model. She has put in some of her own money, based on a valuation of equity that we agreed on and she brings some valuable retail experience as a former senior executive in a women's fashion chain."

Dave's turn, "I'm having no luck yet finding a strategic partner to help me grow to the next level, but I am developing my network and building stronger connections that might get me there. In other news, we are really excited about our new product line. It's a series of upscale cruising bikes for fashion and design conscious women that are not yet cycling, but will find these appealing, I'm sure."

"By upscale, you mean expensive?" asked Paul.

"Yes," replied Dave, "our target customer is upper-middle income, only mildly committed to fitness or cycling, but very attracted to fashion and design. Someone who buys the high priced workout clothes and shoes, but never goes to the gym. They already spend a lot on Lululemon and Nike and other high-end brand names; why not get them on our bikes? Early response in the U.S. has been very good."

"A good example of carefully choosing your target market and going for a niche that is not yet developed. We'll look forward to learning more from your experience," I added.

"Same old, same old for me," said Paul, "but maybe I can find a niche for machined parts that will appeal to those upscale women."

"That may require a little more brainstorming," laughed Stan, who was chairing the meeting, "you can add it to the agenda when you're next in the **Member Spotlight**."

"I'll keep it in mind," said Paul, "but for today..., I have an offer to buy my business, that is a bigger priority."

"Whoa, now you have our attention!"

"It's a competitor, sort of, but for them it's an interesting acquisition. They do not have a shop here now; they're based in Toronto so this would give them new customers and new production capacity with some specialty equipment they don't have. They haven't said no to my 'reasonable' price yet; they are digging deep into the numbers under NDA (an important term I've learned in the process, for Non-Disclosure Agreement). I'll have more news next meeting."

"It sounds like a good prospect for you, Paul. Good luck with the negotiations."

**What have we done for you lately?**

Continuing around the table, next up was Brian. He said, "No such thing as *same old, same old* in our business. The development software keeps requiring updates; security is a continuous challenge to prevent spamming and hacking of our clients' sites; and the creative Web marketing gurus keep coming up with new ways to attract customers. Everybody talks about social media, but not many small business customers do it well and they don't have the budgets to beat the big brand names. We just have to get better at the guerrilla marketing tactics."

"What do you mean by *guerrilla marketing*?" asked Vivian.

"It's not unique to Web marketing," said Brian, "it just means doing something unexpected or outrageous to get attention for your brand or company. To quote Uncle Ralph, '*Guerrilla marketing beats the gorilla every time*'. Meaning that getting on the front page with a photo and headline is always better than the full-page ad that a big brand name paid for. Richard Branson is the best at it and says he couldn't afford to compete otherwise. Have you noticed how often he makes the news for

*Virgin Group* with an event or outrageous stunt that gets your attention?"

"In that case I already do it!" said Vivian. "We are often in the local paper for pet rescue or adopt-a-pet events and advocate for pet health care and good animal nutrition – always with very photogenic cute kittens and puppies. On the other hand, we have to be careful not to venture into the 'pet activist' arena which is not always so well received."

"We're back to the sales tactics of being persistent and persuasive, without being annoying or obnoxious" I said. "It's also important to keep your guerrilla marketing consistent with your strategic positioning and corporate image. Richard Branson has established the *Virgin* brand as being innovative, fun-loving, friendly and value-oriented and so he consistently maintains that image without high cost marketing campaigns. You can do the same for your business."

"Last one up is me," said Stan, "It's been an interesting Roundtable. So I'm sorry I don't have something more exciting for you. No air conditioners for upscale women and nobody has offered to buy my business. No good headline material at all."

"But, I do have some good news. My senior tech and project manager has said he is willing to become a part-owner. We are establishing a process for him to acquire equity over time and I think he could actually do better than me at eventually running the business. I am starting to think about my exit strategy!"

The Member Roundtable was complete and proved again to be a valuable part of the e2eForum meeting. In the quiet confidential, non-competitive forum of peers everyone was comfortable sharing their stories and learning from each other. It always takes a while to establish that level of confidence in each other, but it is well worth developing and maintaining. The Wrap-up Roundtable is a good way to end the e2eForum meetings.

So we were done until next time, but we hope you can join us at another e2eForum meeting again soon.

# 13

## More from Uncle Ralph for Entrepreneurs

In the preceding chapters I have presented some important ideas for entrepreneurs through the discussions in e2eForum meetings. In this chapter I share more ideas for entrepreneurs that I have presented previously in articles, Blogs and other forums.

Let's start with my approach to Business Plans.

You can, of course, buy or borrow a copy of my book *The Complete Do-It-Yourself Guide to Business Plans*, but as a bonus with this book, here is a short summary of my approach on how to write a Business Plan that delivers the results you want.

### *You have to have a Business Plan – for the process, not the product*

Every business needs one. It's not just for start-ups or new product launches or business expansion initiatives.

**Why?**

Documenting a Business Plan is an extremely useful process to focus management and owners on their business concept, their strategies and operating plans. It forces consensus and decision making that might otherwise be neglected. It requires issues to be resolved and the decisions to be reflected in the financial projections.

A well-documented business plan will help you communicate the most important elements of your strategy and plans to the people who need to know them. Including you.

Already in business for years and never needed a business plan? It's still a good idea for all the same reasons. And now is a good time.

Ready to exit your business? Even better. A solid business plan will be the most important document in supporting the valuation of your business.

The greatest value of a business plan, however, is likely to be in the process – involving your management team in a thorough examination of your business – its purpose, its strategies and its plans to ensure success. When completed, all the key players will be more knowledgeable of the issues, the opportunities and the risks and the alternative paths considered before committing to the final plan.

### Layout and Content

Following is a suggested guideline of the layout and content for developing an effective Business Plan. It is a consolidation of best practices, based on my consulting and management experience with many different clients in a wide range of businesses at all stages from their start-up to their exit strategies.

**COVER PAGE:**
Includes title, date, purpose, prepared by whom, confidentiality statement, issued to whom, and a document control number.

**PURPOSE:**
Objectives of the Business Plan – to attract financing, key executives, customers, or strategic partners? To document strategy and action plans for all participants? To set the financial objectives and timetable?

## CONTENTS:

1. **Executive Summary** (Max. 2 pages, written last as a stand-alone document; may be offered for review prior to full disclosure of the business plan; convinces the reader to go further or not.)
   - Business Concept, Plan and Objectives
   - Current status relative to the market opportunity
   - Key success factors, risks, expected results
   - Financial situation and needs
   - Reference to the complete Business Plan for more detail

2. **Concept and Business Opportunity** (Describe the need being addressed; how the approach is different and why it is likely to succeed.)
   - Market need and current solutions available
   - Business concept and product/service differentiation
   - Initial market feedback

3. **Mission statement** (Generate missionaries!, Why should others join the cause – to have fun, make money, make a difference?)
   - Clear, attractive objectives – who and what do you want to be?
   - Statement of values and priorities
   - Milestones and timetable

4. **Market Analysis** (Provide relevant, pertinent information to demonstrate your knowledge and competence in the industry.)
   - The overall market, recent changes
   - Market segments
   - Target market and customers
   - Customer characteristics
   - Customer needs
   - Buying and selling process

5. **Competition** (Demonstrate an awareness of competitors and confirm your ability to compete successfully.)
   - Industry overview, recent changes
   - Nature of competition, inside and outside the industry
   - Primary competitors

- Competitive products/services, relative pricing, advantages, disadvantages
- Opportunities, protection by patents, copyrights, barriers to entry
- Threats and risks, ability of competitors to respond, imitate or copy.

6. **Strategic Plan** (Describe your starting point, direction, objectives and the plan to get there.)
   - Company history and background – experience, resources
   - Key competitive strengths & current weaknesses
   - Business plan and strategy to leverage your strengths and reduce the weaknesses
   - Step-by-step Action Plan for implementing the strategy

7. **Management team** (Usually the most important factor in determining your success and in attracting staff and financing. Emphasize your current strengths and your plan to fill in the gaps.)
   - Key personnel, experience & credentials
   - Staffing plan
   - Organizational structure

8. **Product & Service Offering** (Consider the reader's familiarity with the industry, avoid technical jargon; relate to the market and the competition.)
   - Product/service description
   - Positioning of products/services
   - Competitive evaluation of products/services
   - Future products/services

9. **Marketing and sales plan** (Another key to success, too often neglected by owner/managers with strong product, technical, or operations backgrounds. Prove you have a plan that will be affordable and effective.)
   - Marketing strategy, positioning, presentation
   - Advertising, Promotions/incentives
   - Sales tactics
   - Publicity, public relations, press releases
   - Trade shows, industry events
   - Web marketing

10. **Operations plan** (Describe the important issues and factors that will affect customer service perceptions and the required investments in operations.)
    - Processes for product/service delivery
    - Customer service and support
    - Facilities and staff required

11. **Risk analysis** (What can go wrong, what will you do about it?)
    - Market risks – economic cycle, interest rates, currency, government regulations, trade restrictions.
    - Business risks – key customer & supplier dependence, labour availability, staff turnover, new competitors, new technology, changing demand.

12. **Financial plan** (Convert all the preceding words into numbers, next year by month, then three-to-five years annually.)
    - Summary paragraph and with financial graphics
    - Assumptions and disclaimers
    - Starting Balance Sheet
    - Profit and Loss Projection
    - Cash Flow Projection
    - Balance Sheet Projection
    - Ratio's and Analysis, Value of equity
    - Financial needs
    - Sources of funds

**APPENDICES:**
Add some personalization and realism with biographies and photos of key executives, product photos, marketing literature, sample packaging, facility plans, press releases, customer testimonials, relevant research documents, etc.

Following these guidelines will ensure that you have considered all the issues and can defend your strategies and action plans against all inquisitors.

## Consultants: How to choose, use, and not abuse them
© 2009

Since doing my first consulting project over thirty years ago, I have learned a lot about how to successfully manage consulting projects and the client/consultant relationship. Here are some ideas that may help you with your consultants (and your lawyers, accountants and other professionals):

1. Before you introduce consultants to the process, be sure you **need** what you want and **want** what you need. Beware of consultants that agree to do whatever you want, whether you need it or not.

2. Look internally to confirm the three "C's" of consulting project readiness: **Capacity** in budget, time and resources; **Commitment** of management and staff affected by the process; and **Capability** to support the project and implement the conclusions.

3. One more "C" – **Compatibility.** Select your consultants from an organisation that is compatible with yours - are you a corporate multinational or a local entrepreneurial business?

4. Recognize whether your consulting needs are **strategic** - requiring outside expertise to inspire and facilitate your business planning process or **operational** - bringing knowledge, skills and experience that are not available internally.

5. Meet the **operating consultant.** It may not be the same charming, talented person that sold you the work. And at those fee rates you don't want to train a recent MBA, who started last week and studied your industry yesterday.

6. **Test Drive:** Check whether the consultant arrives with questions, not answers; will operate as neither boss nor employee; and will win the hearts and minds of your staff.

*More from Uncle Ralph for Entrepreneurs*

Successful consultants will listen, understand, empathize, analyze, strategize and persuade better than normal people.

7. Remember you are hiring a consultant to **challenge and push** you. You are not renting a friend to tell you how smart you are.

8. Can you confidently expect a solution that will be **yours** not theirs?

9. Ask for **references.** Call them.

10. Ask **who** is not on the reference list and **why not.** Learn what they think causes a project to be unsuccessful. And ask which list you can expect to be on when this is over.

11. Ask for fee rates and a work plan with estimated hours. Then agree on a **fixed fee** for agreed deliverables with dates, documents and milestones.

12. Don't let their **progress reports** interfere with your progress. Get what you need, not what they need for CYA (*Cover Your A___*) requirements.

13. Check **who else** is billing time to your project. Sometimes there is a very expensive partner back at the office who needs to keep his billing rate up. Your budget can be quickly consumed while he "supervises" from a distance.

14. Avoid **surprises**. Ask about additional expenses: travel, telephone and printing. Terms of payment?

15. Do they have a satisfaction guarantee?

16. Get the agreement in writing, **read it** before signing it.

17. Watch for **signs of trouble**: such as, selling more work before the work is done; long delays between on-site visits; too much time spent "back at the office" and billed to you.

18. And finally, remember consultants are people too. They want to boast about good work and satisfied clients. You can help them help you. **Don't be difficult.**

With all due respect and best regards to all my favourite clients and consultants.

*More from Uncle Ralph for Entrepreneurs*

# *Managing in Difficult Times*
© 2008

Ignoring or avoiding a difficult business environment is simply not possible. It will happen, sooner or later.

A credit crisis, stock market meltdown, or a looming recession all affect the attitudes and actions of consumers, employees, investors, lenders and business managers. What are some helpful ideas to respond effectively?

**Stay focused**

Avoid being distracted by the bombardment of bad news. Stay focused on customers and employees, especially the ones that you have and want to keep. Don't freeze. But don't over-react. Be calm, rational, reassuring and pro-active. Don't just share the pain, provide relief. Misery may love company, but everybody still remains miserable, if you just talk about it and do nothing. Try to be more creative and take appropriate action. Don't neglect the good news; look for the silver lining in the dark clouds – maybe the exchange and interest rates are down, so now you can expedite foreign currency sales or re-finance some lending to improve cash flow.

**Be relevant**

Take a close look at your customers' changing needs and your product or service offerings. Do you have recession proof products or are they vulnerable? Costumers will be postponing or redirecting their purchase decisions in the current climate. Can you keep their business with a new cost-reduced service or more creative approach to packaging, pricing, terms and conditions?

**Leverage the sense of urgency**

Nobody is unaware of the current economic circumstances affecting your business. Employees are already aware of the issues and the problems in front of them, so it will be easier to get them to accept the solutions. That means more likely that they are receptive to expense reductions, removing frills, postponing projects, reducing assets and conserving cash. It may be opportune to revise compensation or bonus plans, change distribution channels, move marketing programs to lower cost Internet approaches. Take advantage of the sense of urgency that exists. Now is the time to resolve lingering problems; just be cautious not to do permanent damage to key employee, customer and supplier relationships that you want to retain.

### Recognize the changing environment

You probably started the year under different assumptions that affected corporate budgets and compensation plans. Sales targets may now be unrealistic and should be adjusted downwards to maintain the rewards and motivation for top performers who continue to deliver in spite of challenging times. Try to use an external benchmark to justify the adjustment and not give the impression that you are forgiving poor performance.

### Look for opportunities generated by the crisis

If you have been smart enough to stash cash and build a relatively secure business, then you can take advantage of some unique opportunities that exist. Build your team by attracting top performing employees who may be ready to move from shaky competitors into your welcoming arms. Or take out a competitor if the company is suddenly for sale at a bargain price. The big boys are doing it; so can you.

### Talk to your banker

Make sure she is not worrying unnecessarily. Or at least worrying for the right reasons and hearing them directly from you. If you are in better shape than most and credit is available, then increase your credit limits now to handle the potential unexpected impacts and to support the new opportunities you may want to pursue.

**Avoid being the unwilling prey**

Recognize that competitors may also see you in difficulty and seize the opportunity to raid key employees or buy you out at a bargain price. You need to keep close to your key employees and ensure their career plans remain with you. If you are a likely target for merger or acquisition, then start working on your choice of preferred partner and determine your business valuation under normal circumstances, not distress pricing. Then take the initiative before you lose control of the situation.

In summary: be brave, be flexible, and be creative. Analyze, decide, and take action. You and your business will be better for it.

# E-Business Challenges for Entrepreneurs

It would unacceptable I'm sure, to write a book of advice for entrepreneurs without discussing the impact of the Internet and Web technologies on small business. So this section is meant to avoid that potential deficiency.

Since the early stages of the internet era, most small businesses have been trying to figure out how, or if, it applied to them. Like the social media issues of today. As I had some early experience with the Internet and Web applications I have been able to provide advice and direction to entrepreneurs and managers from traditional "old economy" businesses that were evaluating the potential opportunities for their businesses.

Following is a collection of some of my articles and ideas on e-business that were useful in providing input for those entrepreneurs and they may still be instructive for you now. Enjoy the read and reflect on how much has changed in such a short period of time and how much has remained the same.

# THE FIRST STEP – Getting Started
© 2000

Feeling behind the times because you are not using the Internet in your business? Don't be embarrassed, you are not yet the last to sign on.

In spite of all the media attention and the hard sell from Internet service and equipment providers, a recent survey indicated that although 70% of U.S. small businesses are currently connected, only 38% have Web sites. Probably even fewer in Canada.

But before you get too comfortable you should also recognize that the Internet has changed the world around you and that small businesses are the most vulnerable. They are going to be caught in the cross fire between the aggressive Internet initiatives of larger corporations that can make huge resource commitments and the brash young entrepreneurs that are boldly launching new business models to replace the old economy. You cannot afford to keep your head down and wait.

It's time to get started. Never mind the justification – whether it's cool, your competitors are doing it, your customers want it, or your ego is pushing you – just accept the inevitability of this technology affecting your business. The risks are real and the opportunities are immense. Even though current business volumes in the Internet economy are relatively small, the growth rates are astonishing – from zero to 50 million Internet users in the first four years. There are now over 150 million users in North America plus 87 million in Western Europe and 72 million in the Asia Pacific region. By 2005, these figures are expected to be 230 million, 213 million, and 189 million, respectively. Knowledgeable and aggressive marketers like Procter & Gamble are rapidly shifting their targets to the online audience.

So carefully assess both the opportunities and the implications, and then develop an action plan to get your business online.

### Start with the learning process

Get educated on the nature of the Web and the potential for your business. It simply takes an Internet connection and the time to explore. Visit the players in your own industry, but learn from other good sites as well as the ones that turn you off. Then do an assessment of your own situation. Is your interest in business-to-consumer or business-to-business? Consider your employees, customers and suppliers. Are they connected and comfortable with the Internet? Make sure the key staff in your business are also aware of the opportunities and the requirements to succeed with e-commerce.

### Keep your focus on business objectives

It is easy to be dazzled by the technology or the growth statistics. But the opportunities offered by electronic commerce should be assessed against the same business criteria you use for other investments. Any Internet initiative can be a painful and expensive exercise. Be sure it is justified by the impact on increasing sales, reducing costs, improving customer service, or enhancing competitive advantage. The goals need to be clear in order to keep up your nerve during the process.

Once the opportunities are identified, develop more specific objectives including a budget and implementation schedule. Don't try to do it all in the first step. Focus on one key area and do it well, rather than launching several tentative, incomplete efforts. Develop a plan for your Web site to evolve through the stages from presentation, to interaction, to transactions. Decide to what extent and at what stage you will integrate the Web processes into existing operating systems.

Do not start until you have a clear understanding and a commitment to the plan from everyone affected by the Internet strategy.

### Management issues go beyond the technology

Before the opportunities can be realized a number of important implications must be addressed by management. These may be described as commitment, capacity and capability. Is the project supported by all the affected management and staff? Do you have the time and financial resources? Are you capable of installing and maintaining the new technology?

Outside resources will likely be required in addition to assigning responsibility internally. Use experienced and competent experts, even though it will be more expensive than using your nephew or another enthusiastic volunteer. Their learning experience will show up in your Web site as an amateurish token effort; and it is too important for that.

There will also be new obligations to provide training and systems support, to promote your Web site, to respond to new customer demands, and to ensure Internet security. Be sure to install reporting and analysis processes to monitor and respond with the necessary changes to achieve your original objectives.

**If you missed the target, adjust, reload, and fire again**

Nobody gets it right the first time, so accept the fact that this is still a learning experience for everybody. Don't be intimidated by those who are just one short chapter ahead of you. If you've done your homework, you will probably have avoided some mistakes that they did not.

But there will be surprises. You may find that your initial objective was to increase sales into new markets, but the biggest opportunity turns out to be better service at lower costs for current customers. Be prepared for inquiries from places you have no ability to supply. Expect your current distribution channel to over-react and to worry about your selling directly from a Web site. Respond quickly and clearly because misinformation can spread very quickly. Keep your own staff well informed about your plans, the results, and the process to integrate Web activities into existing operations.

Once your site is up and running satisfactorily, step way back and re-evaluate the plan and the results against your new realities.

Consider changing your objectives and exploiting the new economy with some completely different ways of doing business. Do some brainstorming and develop some radical new options before launching the next step.

*More from Uncle Ralph for Entrepreneurs*

# THE NEXT STEP - Doing it better.
© 2000

So now you have a Web site, but as Shania Twain might say, "it don't impress me much". Don't be discouraged, it's a common feeling after the first attempt at joining the Internet economy.

It is easy to spend a lot of time, effort and money to launch a Web site and still accomplish very little. But don't give up and write off the investment. Extract as much as possible from the learning experience. And give yourself credit for not ignoring the New Economy. At least you are trying to participate in the Internet gold rush that seems to be happening exactly 100 years after the original Klondike. Then too, a lot of brave souls suffered pain and hardship to be part of the adventure and get their share of the wealth.

To succeed with the next step up your own Chilkoot Trail to Internet glory let's look back and learn from the experience up to this point. Were your objectives and plan clear from the start? Were you committed to the plan and to the resources required? Did you ignore the obstacles and resistance from affected employees, customers, and channel partners, instead of resolving them in advance? Could the negative feedback have been prevented? Can you now build on this experience to deliver better results?

Remember the Internet is like baseball and golf - it's not good enough to swing and hope. You have to study, prepare, train, practice, and do it a lot before you get good at it. So now that the first step is behind you let's move on to the next step - doing it better.

**It's more than the wrong choice of graphics and colour**

What is the source of your discontent? Aside from the time and money invested, where exactly have the results been disappointing? No visitors? Too little activity? Or just negative feedback? Be willing to ignore the amateur critics who will happily give you their opinion on the look and feel of your site. But pay attention if there is strong consensus that says your site is badly designed, too slow, or hard to navigate. That is valuable input that can be used to make fixes and confirm that you are committed to your e-commerce strategy and that you appreciate your customers' input.

**Was it the wrong destination or the wrong route?**

After reviewing feedback and the site analysis reports, it's time to re-think the original objectives and the plan. Do they need revision? Should you be more ambitious, aggressive, even radical? Or should you just get the bugs out and fine tune before adding more functionality or content.

Your objectives should have a primary focus on one of the key success criteria: increasing sales, reducing costs, improving customer service, or enhancing corporate image. If progress is being made then you are on the right track. Increasing activity may be simply a matter of pumping up the marketing effort, both online and in the traditional channels.

**Evolve with your customers**

The Internet has become a key resource in developing the customer relationship. Customer expectations have evolved. The early attraction of customers may have been based on low price and good service. That may not be sufficient to retain the customer when he or she is promised a lower price and better service somewhere else. Customer loyalty will be developed when there is also an appreciation of the additional value of your knowledge, experience and competence. But the most valuable long-term customer relationship arises when there is a strong trust arising from personal experience and recognition of shared beliefs, attitudes, and values.

This level of customer relationship can be enhanced through your Web site. It cannot be automated. (No software or animated sales robot will ever replace a friendly customer service phone call or a visit from a knowledgeable, reliable sales person.) But your Web site should reflect more than your products, prices, and service policies. It should reflect your corporate personality. Is it cute and perky, or calm and professional?

The technology and techniques of the Internet should be used in the same fashion you would direct your staff to deal with customers. Polite and persuasive sales people, not aggressive or annoying. Friendly and helpful customer service representatives, not young renegades lost in their own funky, high tech world.

The abuse of e-mail marketing can also make you as unpopular as the guy that sent the LOVE BUG virus around the world. Online customers have learned to appreciate the approach of permission marketing. It is as simple as explaining why you would like to have any personal information and how you will use it, and then asking for permission to send a newsletter, promotions or product information via e-mail, or regular mail.

**Continue to monitor, adjust, and develop**

The value of an online presence is in the continuous and instantaneous feedback. Continue to monitor activity and performance in order to respond before bottlenecks occur. Adjust your targets and your methods to exploit the opportunities as they are presented. Launch new initiatives with a rigorous, disciplined approach to planning and project management.

You may not strike the mother lode, but you will pick up a few nuggets and avoid starving to death.

# Lessons learned from an e-commerce adventure
© 2000

It is better to have tried and failed than never to have tried at all; and even more important to learn from your mistakes.

That is what I keep telling myself after having invested the time and cash equivalent to a Harvard MBA in an e-commerce start-up that has stalled and is winding down. Not a happy prospect in light of all the media pre-occupation with e-commerce success stories and the young millionaires watching their IPOs rocket into cyberspace. But the headlines ignore the more frequent stories of new e-commerce businesses that do not hit the stock market jackpot. Many of them either settle into a low-key niche or exhaust their resources and fold.

This is the story of an Internet venture that did not make the headlines, but offers some useful insights for entrepreneurs evaluating their own initiatives. The lessons learned are applicable to your own new venture or to an investment in someone else's.

In mid-1998 we launched a new company called nxtNet (www.nxtnet.com) with the slogan ... "taking you to the next level on the Internet".

My partner and I both had prior successful entrepreneurial experience in computer products and wanted to start a new venture together. We decided to develop a business that would catch the next wave of e-commerce services for mid-sized companies seeking to do business on the Internet. After long discussions, searches for a unique service offering, and many draft business plans, we developed a market strategy and then chose Intershop Communications as our software development platform. This product had the advantages of being suitable for single or multiple online storefronts, and offered a flexible, economic and comprehensive solution. We committed to the product, staffing, facilities and equipment to start training and development immediately. The two of us provided the time and cash required to get started.

*More from Uncle Ralph for Entrepreneurs*

By October 1998, we had an initial product with application as an online storefront for an associated computer business. At the same time, we realized that the application had wide appeal to other computer dealers and could be sold as a multi-user database service and e-commerce resource. We had developed a consolidated catalogue of 85,000 computer products from multiple distributor product databases that allowed rapid search and comparison for product information, pricing, and current sources. Users could access the catalogue from the Internet and find a product by manufacturer, category, and part number, key word or price range and immediately see the alternate sources and prices with links to more technical information, preferred dealer pricing and actual stock levels. Additional features allowed the catalogue to be customized so that any computer reseller could present the database as his own online storefront. This option offered all the search and product information features to his customers and enabled online ordering at his suggested retail pricing.

The product offering quickly received positive feedback and strong indications of support from all the participants – resellers, distributors, and manufacturers. It was a comprehensive, powerful, and effective tool for buying and selling at all levels within the Canadian computer distribution channel. Resellers recognized the value in an online resource to save time and effort. Distributors and manufacturers saw the opportunity to promote their products, and major publishers in the industry wanted to offer complementary online services to their subscribers and advertisers. How could we fail with all this enthusiasm and support?

While the potential for success clearly existed, everybody had the same questions and reservations – "Who is there now?" "How many are using it?" and "I don't want to pay until it's bigger".

Reasonable objections we thought, so we added features and content for free. We promoted the product with free trials and low cost subscriptions for reseller access. Then we coaxed, persuaded, sold hard, and made deals. The "contra" became the standard for obtaining press coverage, free ads, mailing lists and promotion in exchange for free participation and future consideration. Activity on the Web site and catalogue grew to 3000 visitors per month with over 800 subscribers and the distributor list increased from three to twelve.

But revenue remained near zero as most reseller subscribers declined to pay for the service. Reasons were "it should be free - let the advertisers pay", "I don't use it enough", "there are lower cost options", or "we built our own solution". The audience did not grow fast enough even after we offered it for free, to satisfy the advertisers and content providers. Without persistent and conspicuous sales and marketing efforts, all the participants quickly lost interest. Meanwhile the costs of database maintenance, ongoing development, site hosting, Internet access, sales, marketing, and administration were increasing.

Clearly the old entrepreneurial model of controlling costs and growing revenue was not going to apply. We had to realign our profile to show how zero revenue and high initial costs could still lead to significant investment returns like other well-known Internet ventures. So from early 1999 we started an aggressive search for financing, estimating our requirements at $500,000 to $1,500,000 over the next two years before achieving positive cash flow. More business plans, spreadsheets, and glossy presentations to demonstrate future valuations up to $20 million, even $40 million.

We knocked on many doors, from banks to government agencies, from angel investors to venture capital, from stock promoters to business consultants, and again received lots of encouragement, but no financing. So, as founding partners were faced with a continuing cash drain, no relief in sight, and the limits of our own resources rapidly approaching. It was time to put the project on hold. Strategic partners or investors might still be developed to proceed with the project, but the ongoing expenditures were stopped in late 1999.

So what were the lessons learned? We already knew that nothing ventured, nothing gained. We now also knew that big successes in the new economy require big investments. Entrepreneurs may start small, but large investments will be required from new sources to achieve significant success. And no one will put significant money into a venture unless it is the only remaining requirement.

The concept, product, development, marketing and staffing all have to be in place before an investor will provide the final ingredient – his cash. Exceptions are likely only where the management team has already succeeded in the same arena, or the investor himself can deliver the missing elements, such as customers or management skills. No investor is going to take the chance that the entrepreneur with a good concept or product will also be able to deliver the required management and marketing skills to succeed after he has the cash.

Next time we will know better. And there are side benefits from this expensive learning experience. I can now admit that with the knowledge gained through our association with Intershop Communications, I was confident enough to make an investment in their stock on the German Neue Markt at 65 Euros last year. It went over 400 Euros last month and is still rising with their rapid growth and the prospect of a NASDAQ listing this year. Almost enough to recover my investment in nxtNet.

So the most important lesson is that education in the new economy is essential and not free, but it can lead to success outside the original plan. Learn, be aware, and be aggressively opportunistic.

# Lessons Learned from Both Sides of the Digital Divide
© 2007

I have learned some important lessons from my experience on both sides of the digital divide – as a peddler of technology services and as a client of technology providers. In the new world of the Web and E-commerce opportunities these lessons are important to keep in mind:

1. The first wave of Internet investment was driven by fear and greed.

2. Current e-business plans require more than a bright idea and a high "burn rate".

3. Success requires a strategy and a plan before jumping into action.

4. People and supporting processes are <u>always</u> more important than the technology.

5. Cool technology is a distraction; focus on the business objectives - sales increases, cost reductions, service improvements, and enhanced corporate image.

6. **The secret of success is to turn the WWW upside down: Think MMM: Management, Marketing, Monitoring.**

7. Stop worrying about what your Web site <u>looks like</u>, start worrying about what it <u>does</u>.

8. Focus less on what it costs and more on how it pays.

9. You cannot automate <u>outstanding</u> customer service – it requires the personal touch of real people.

10. No matter how good the product is, it <u>never</u> sells itself.

11. E-mail marketing works if it's welcome to the reader; don't be a SPAMMER.

12. Viral marketing works even better: "Try it, tell a friend, win a prize."

13. Guerrilla marketing works better than gorilla marketing. (Getting attention on the front page will beat a full-page ad every time.)

14. When cash is short and you can't find OPM (Other People's Money), try contra deals. (Exchange your products and services for other consideration, without exchanging cash.)

15. It's easier to get outside financing if you don't need anything else.

16. Beware of unwilling and unwelcome partners. Look for intelligent and sympathetic capital.

17. Be patient in the search for investors. Expect many "No's" before getting to a "Yes".

18. Remember the risks are real, but the opportunities are huge. (i.e. We're still driven by fear and greed.)

# E-business Opportunities with Web 2.0
© 2009

In our mission at DirectTech Solutions to advise, inform and inspire business owners and managers, we offer these ideas for your consideration.

**Have you been neglecting the e-business opportunities for your business?**

In the early days of the Internet and e-business solutions the message was to "Catch the wave or be drowned by it". Every business was being told to get on the Internet to survive or stand back while the "new economy" took over their industry. Hype and hysteria were used to persuade entrepreneurs and investors to put large amounts of money into their e-business initiatives. They were motivated by either fear or greed.

Then the "old economy" rules hit the dot.com ventures and the bubble burst. Many investments ended badly. Some could be written off as an expensive learning experience. Some were just bad investments. The hype and hysteria died and many businesses decided they could go back to business as usual. **They were wrong.**

The Internet revolution continues, albeit more quietly. The hype now focuses on **Web 2.0** with highly interactive web sites and user generated content. Huge values are being placed on high traffic sites as they are acquired by Google, Microsoft, or the media moguls, but you don't have to be a media or Web-based business to take advantage of Web 2.0.

*The businesses that are leveraging the new Internet most effectively are those that simply take advantage of Web marketing to attract business and use online services to build strong loyal customer relationships.*

Those are the e-business opportunities not to be neglected. Here are some ideas to consider for using the new Internet in your business:

1. Try a search to see what a potential new customer will find if she *"Googles"* your name, your company or your brand name. You may discover, like I did when shopping for a new BBQ that the most popular site is one full of customer complaints about "a dangerous piece of trash nobody should ever buy!" How would you like that to be the first impression for a new prospect? Or maybe you'll find a comment like the time I checked a hotel on tripadvisor.com and read "put a fork in your eye before booking this hotel!" So be sure you know what potential buyers are finding through search engines. It may give you an incentive to improve the search ranking of the sites that you would prefer they find.
2. Remember that *search engine marketing* is more than putting keywords on your site and hoping to be found by new customers. Optimizing your web site for search engine effectiveness is a complex process and it is worthwhile to consult an expert. If the most common search terms are dominated by bigger competitors, the most effective strategy may be to target a very specific market niche that is not already over-served by competing Web sites. Or use geo-targeting to focus on your local market.
3. Also consider *sponsoring carefully selected keywords* that will deliver interested prospects. People searching for those keywords are motivated potential buyers. Again there are many issues to assess, but you can start with a small budget and learn from the results to continuously improve the performance.
4. You may also want to *monitor and participate* in some of those sites that talk about products like yours and add your own two cents worth. Just be careful to maintain integrity speaking for yourself or your company. Do not make the mistake of pretending to be a delighted customer. Others have already experienced that PR disaster.
5. Many of the new Web 2.0 oriented sites attract very focused groups of site visitors who actively participate in the site. Some of them may align very well with your target market and be very productive for your placement of *relevant online advertising*. For example, if your target market is young Canadian women then look at Divine.ca.

6. ***What about a Blog?*** A personal diary on the Web is probably not helpful to your business unless you are already a celebrity. But you may want to make yourself ***more visible and available*** and to establish yourself ***as an expert resource.*** Both objectives can contribute to building stronger customer relationships. A Blog site will also improve your search engine rankings if it reinforces the same keywords and is linked to your company site and others that are relevant. It does impose the obligation though to keep adding new content. See my Blog and links to others for some ideas. Or try it yourself at Blogger.com.
7. Maybe you should create a ***Blog for your customers?*** Setting up an online users group might be helpful to exchange ideas and input while creating a higher level of brand loyalty and commitment.
8. Also consider Web 2.0 applications to ***reduce your costs and improve your services***. The available applications have evolved to deliver more for less. Powerful and easy-to-use sales force automation and email marketing services are available from providers like Salesforce.com and ConstantContact.
9. Your ***customers and employees*** may be very comfortable with all the latest applications - Blogs, social networks, user generated content, RSS feeds, Pod casting, Tags, Twitter, and Wikis. Their ***expectations are high.*** Can you productively integrate any of these applications into your e-business strategy? If you do not, is there a risk that a competitor or a new approach will lead customers away from you?

Much has changed on the Internet, but neglecting it is not an option.

***Remember fear and greed still apply***

You will have noticed that the sermon on e-business from me or anyone else has not changed much in fifteen years. Essentially, be aware of the possibilities; keep up with customer expectations; have a plan that is appropriate to your budget, capabilities and business model; then do it.

Those principles apply whether you are finally upgrading your first website are you are now trying to enhance your online performance with a social media campaign.

In summary, although Internet technologies and applications have evolved incredibly in the twenty years since we first connected and in the ten years since Facebook started, the sound management principles for applying the Web to your business still apply.

The Internet names and numbers may have changed, but the advice has not:

- Your online initiatives must be an integral part of your business plan.
- Thorough preparation and good project management are essential to achieving a satisfactory return for your online investments.
- Continuously monitoring the real-time feedback and analytics will allow you to review, respond and revise your plans for improved results.

Start with a diagnostic of your current online performance, check the competitive environment and then come up with a plan to do better.

*Don't Do It the Hard Way*

# Henry Mintzberg is Worth Listening to
© 2009

I recently had the pleasure of hearing a presentation by Henry Mintzberg, McGill professor and management guru. One attendee described him as the "Tiger Woods of management science".

I know him as the Strategy Prof during my McGill MBA of 35 years ago. *(Yikes, neither of us seem to have aged that much! OK, greyer for me and less hair for him.)*

He is a widely respected academic and the acclaimed author of "The Nature of Managerial Work ", "The Rise and Fall of Strategic Planning", "Managers not MBAs" and many other books and articles that argue against the conventional wisdom and provoke thoughtful reflection on management and business. He is also the co-founder of the International Masters Program in Practicing Management (IMPM), a unique approach to learning that is designed to flow from the experience of the participants.

His presentation yesterday was originally advertised to be on the dilemma of corporate compensation, but that turned out be only part of his critique of the modern CEO's focus on shareholder value that was a factor in the great recession of 2008.

Some of his points to consider:
- Productivity is a euphemism for cutting costs, mostly by firing employees ("blood letting"), while maintaining short-term revenues.
- The theoretical corporate objective of maximizing long-term shareholder value has been hijacked to mean pushing short-term earnings to inflate current market share prices.
- How can employees be motivated to work for shareholders they have never met? Many of whom have no interest in the company except for the short-term ability to make a profit on their investment - they are day traders or hedge funds.
- Shareholder value is not a worthy objective of the corporate institution as it specifically ignores (or exploits) other stakeholders, especially employees.

- Mercenary corporate leadership is stealing from shareholders with absurd compensation and severance packages that are not tied to performance. The "robber barons are back!"
- The old corporate silos have been replaced by horizontal slabs of concrete separating executives from their employees and the real operating issues.
- "Human resources" is a term that dehumanizes human beings. It makes it easier to treat people like other "resources" to buy, sell, use and dispose of them. It's like describing airline passengers as "self-loading cargo"!
- Corporations need to remember that customers are people too. They are not just another asset to be exploited.

Professor Mintzberg also suggested some remedies to avoid another recession like we had in 2008:
- Stop being misled by the apparent productivity gains and profitability of large American corporations.
- Get the mercenaries out of the executive suite and add employee voices in the boardroom.
- Stop running businesses to satisfy financial analysts or investors with no interest in anything except short-term results.
- Install real corporate leadership that is concerned, engaged, and modest. (*Interestingly close to Jim Collins description of Level 5 Leadership from "Good to Great".*)
- Ignore the obsession with measurable factors and reconsider the immeasurable - values, benefits and impacts of economic activity.
- In the larger context, get back to a better balance of the three sectors in society - public, private and social.

His full commentary and other thought-provoking ideas and analysis are available at *Mintzberg.org*

Lots to think about and to influence if we can.

*Don't Do It the Hard Way*

## The Best Advice I Ever Got

In three words: DON'T WASTE TIME.

Providing the following background story may appear to be an example of not following that advice; me taking the time to write more and you taking the time to read it. But the advice is really about making choices on how to use the limited time available in one lifetime. It does not exclude learning, relaxing, or quiet contemplation instead of continuous frantic activity. In this case I am choosing to reinforce the message and help make it memorable by telling the story (in keeping with the theme of this book) and you may choose to read it for the same reasons.

I was at UBC in 1964, my first year in Engineering. All first-year engineers were given the *Engineering Handbook* providing all the advice and information we needed to successfully complete the following four years of study. The book was full of useful material and started with welcoming comments from the Dean of Engineering, University President and other dignitaries – with all the usual flowery clichés expected in these publications.

One page was reserved for Steve Whitelaw, President of the University Undergraduate Society. Steve was a popular President with a reputation as a very bright, creative leader. That reputation was based on his leadership in a number of engineering student stunts that made the national news, like the time they kidnapped another university mascot or hung a VW beetle from the Lion's Gate Bridge. His biggest coup was bringing to a conclusion the long campus debate over some weird concrete modern-art sculptures that appeared one year on campus. They had received the scorn and contempt of 'ignorant and uncultured' engineering students, but were vigorously defended by the arts faculty and administration.

The intensity of the debate exploded on campus, and in the local papers, on the day the engineers went on a rampage and completely destroyed all the sculptures leaving them in heaps of broken concrete and steel. That's when Steve confirmed that the engineers had built and installed them all in the first place.

So his advice in the *Engineering Handbook* would have received our attention.

It was a blank page with his signature and the three words:

> DON'T WASTE TIME

Call it leading by example.

# Appendices

## *Guiding Principles of the e2eForum*

As I mentioned in the Introduction, the operating principles for the e2eForum are based on my previous experience with other networking groups, business associations and peer advisory groups.

In this Appendix, I recommend these guidelines for you to use in starting your own e2eForum or to improve the effectiveness of a group that you are already participating in.

**More than Networking**

Most of us have learned the value of a good business or professional network and have promoted our businesses by word-of-mouth marketing through active participation in different networking groups. These groups usually focus on getting to know new friends and influencers that can help you with leads and referrals. Some groups are more aggressive and structured than others and some members are more annoying and less effective than others; but, much like a typical multi-level marketing organization they can be very helpful to a new business looking to expand their list of contacts and prospects. They tend to work best for retail and consumer businesses where all the members of the network can become customers as well as sources of leads and referrals.

Industry and professional associations, chambers of commerce and boards of trade can also be valuable resources to build your contact network. However, the networking objective in these groups is usually less explicitly built into the meetings and the group is consequently less valuable as a place to sell your services or request leads and referrals. You will usually need to be more subtle and patient at introducing yourself and your business while demonstrating your competency and value to other members. Many participants in these groups are turned off by the aggressive networkers insistently promoting their business at every occasion.

## Purpose

The e2eForum is much more than a networking group. You will definitely improve your network of business associates and receive high quality leads and referrals, but the primary purpose in the e2eForum is to learn and share experiences with other entrepreneurs in order to develop better solutions to your common challenges and improve the performance of your business.

These are the guiding principles I recommend for effectively meeting those objectives.

## Participation

Membership in the e2eForum is only by invitation from an existing member who has confidence in the capabilities, integrity and suitability of the new member for participation in the forum.

An existing member has the right of veto to exclude any invited new member, subject only to a required explanation for the inviting member.

Members must all respect the confidentiality of the forum discussions; they must have no personal or business conflict-of-interest; and, they must have no competitive, customer or supplier relationship with any other member.

There are no minimum requirements for time in business, amount of revenue or number of employees. The key criteria are the character of the individual and their ability to contribute to the e2eForum learning and sharing experience.

New members should receive and accept a confirmation of the principles of operation of the e2eForum.

## Group objectives

- Regular interaction with like-minded entrepreneurs who have started or are operating their own business.
- Sharing ideas, information, strategies and operating practices to advance their businesses.
- Developing new business opportunities by exchanging leads and referrals and by direct introduction to new client opportunities.
- Occasional joint efforts to promote their businesses, products and services

## Guiding principles

- Membership is by invitation only, based on a recommendation by an existing member.
- Maximum of 12 members per meeting.
- Members are non-competing entrepreneurs in owner-managed businesses.
- Information and exchanges within the group are treated with discretion and respect for client confidentiality.
- No pressure, no quotas, no score-keeping to exchange referrals, leads or introductions to new business.
- No referral fees between members.

- No obligation to do business between members, recognizing the existence of prior relationships, and no obligation to preferential treatment if members become customers or suppliers of each other. (Both of those results will occur naturally, as members get to know, like, respect and trust each other.)

**Time, Place and Fees**

I recommend morning meetings every three weeks, but alternatively the members may prefer every second week, or only monthly, for example every third Thursday, or first Tuesday of every month. (Generally mid-week morning meetings are better for regular attendance, but if day-care drop off or other duties make mornings impossible, then evenings may work better for some groups.)

- At a convenient hotel or restaurant that can provide breakfast and a quiet private conference room for the meetings. (Sometimes a member can offer the company board room and provide breakfast services.)
- Meeting agenda scheduled from 7:30 – 9:00AM.
- Membership fees billed semi-annually in advance to cover the costs of the conference room, facilities and breakfast.
- Any special events or e2eForum materials can be included in the semi-annual fees or billed as they occur.
- One member should be designated as the group treasurer to manage the billing and fees.

**Agenda**

In order for the meetings to be effective and use the limited time effectively, two things are required: a designated chairperson and an agreed agenda.

I recommend rotating the chairperson among the experienced members every six months (choosing arbitrarily by seniority or alphabetically, since neither voting nor volunteering ever works very well.)

A meeting agenda for the e2eForum may include any or all of the following items, but typically sections are extended or re-scheduled in order to maintain the 90-minute time limit and provide sufficient time for in-depth discussion on particular issues:

1. Welcome and introduction of guests or new members.
2. Confirm the Agenda and Discussion Points for the day.
3. Member Discussion Forum or Guest Presentation (20 - 40 minutes)
4. Member spotlight (20 - 40 minutes) as an alternative to the standard Discussion Forum or Guest Presentation. Getting to know the member better and sharing advice on current challenges or opportunities.
   - Member's business: Products and services, typical clients and projects.
   - Target Market: type of client, business or industry, typical prospect or primary contacts.
   - Current challenges, opportunities?
   - What can we help you with?
5. Member Roundtable - Sharing business updates (1 - 2 minutes each, total 15 - 20 minutes).
   - What's new - clients, mandates, milestones?
   - Current issues.
6. Conclude
   - Follow-up action items.
   - Plan for next meeting.

**Events:**
In addition to the regular meetings, members may also agree to extend their joint efforts to include:

- Meetings on-site of one of the members for the member Spotlight
- Organizing an occasional extended breakfast seminar inviting guests to meet members and demonstrate their expertise by leading the seminar.
- One-on one meetings between members, to develop a closer working relationship and follow-up on any shared opportunities, issues, referrals, leads or other agreed action items.

These guiding principles for operation of the e2eForum will help you to start your own peer advisory group.

You may also follow Uncle Ralph on *www.e2eForum.com* to get more input and suggestions on how to be successful with your group. The following section provides some useful discussion topics for your group.

## Discussion Topics for the e2eForum

In the book we covered a number of important discussion topics that are listed below. These are followed by some other suggestions that will be helpful to facilitate more effective e2eForum discussions among entrepreneur members.

## Discussion Topics from *Don't Do It the Hard Way*

### How to succeed
- When to leap?
- What do you need before you start?
- Who will succeed and who will not?
- Why and why not?

### Start-up Decisions
- Strategic Positioning
- Strategic Partnerships
- Business model choices
- Document requirements

### Too Entrepreneurial
- Opportunistic
- Optimistic
- Impatient
- Confident
- Decisive
- Creative

### The Entrepreneur's Challenge:
- Strategic Leadership + Management Effectiveness

### Serial Entrepreneurship
- Another Start-up?
- Or the next Screw-up?

**Financial Challenges**
- Profit versus Long-term Value
- Managing the Balance Sheet

**Key Relationships**
- Employees before customers
- Biggest before loudest
- Bankers as partners

**Building your Business**
- Goal = Long-term, loyal, profitable customers.
- Process = Marketing + Sales + Customer Service

**Personal Issues**
- Family in or out?
- Employees like family?

**Preparing for exit**
- Establishing business value
- Enhancing business value
- Management succession plans
- Exit strategies

## More Suggested Discussion Topics

**Recently Read: What did you learn?**
- Recommended reading
- Key ideas, principles, recommendations
- How to apply them

**Case Study: Recently in the news**
- Big business failure
- Acquisition for big bucks – why?
- Small business success story
- Current business issues being debated

**Current Business Challenges:**
- Employee participation in business ownership
- Compensation plans, incentives, benefits
- Business development – priorities and budgets
- Using Web marketing and social media
- Social responsibility initiatives

## Check Lists from the e2eForum

During the e2eForum meetings, Uncle Ralph presented a number of useful Checklists.

They are summarized here for your easy reference.

## Characteristics of a Successful Entrepreneur

- Energetic, competitive, independent, confident, persistent, action-oriented, decisive.
- Passionate, persuasive communicator.

## Before you Launch Checklist

- ☐ Skills, knowledge, experience, and contacts relevant to your business plan.
- ☐ Expectations and preferences for the entrepreneurial lifestyle – work routine and environment, prestige and compensation, work/life balance.
- ☐ Personal strengths and weaknesses that will help, not hurt, the business.
- ☐ Healthy foundation – family, physical and financial. Solid or shaky?
- ☐ Strategic resources in place – partners, suppliers, facilities, key customers and employees.
- ☐ Financing for start-up – including your Basic Defensive Interval and the first few months of negative cash flow.

## The Start-up Document Checklist

1. Business Plan.
2. Shareholder agreement.
3. Life insurance on each other.
4. Incorporation.

5. Business licenses and regulatory approvals.
6. Information systems.
7. Leases and contracts for facilities and services.

## *Encore Performance Checklist*

Ask yourself these questions before you get started on your next venture:

- What was it that made you succeed in your first business? Did you build your business on your unique management ability, a new product idea, a preferred customer or supplier relationship? Which of these will apply to the new business?
- What mistakes have you avoided in the past? Are you about to make them now? What new risks are you encountering for the first time?
- Is now a good time to start something new? Are there no challenges left in your current business?
- How much will your current business be impacted by a new initiative and the demands on your time and resources?
- Is your past success really transferable to a new business?

## *Building loyal, long-term, profitable customers*

- All efforts must be dedicated to the *primary objective of every business: building loyal, long-term, profitable customer relationships*
- It's a three-part process of Marketing plus Sales plus Customer Service.

*Customer Experience* should evolve through four levels:

1. Satisfaction with price and availability
2. Recognition of superior service levels
3. Appreciation of the value of your knowledge and experience
4. Connection on values, mission and vision

## The Six P's of Marketing

Build your marketing objectives and plan around the six P's of marketing strategy and product management.

### STRATEGIC:

1. **Positioning:**
   - Strategic positioning of the product relative to competitors in the target market sector will affect all the other elements – placement, promotion, product, pricing, and packaging.
   - Choice of high versus low in quality, price, and service.

2. **Placement:**
   - Where is the product or service available for customers?
   - Choices of retail or wholesale, online or storefront, direct sale or through distributors and sales agents.

3. **Promotion:**
   Choices of priorities, budget and effort in:
   - Direct marketing, advertising.
   - Public relations activities, participation in trade associations, conferences, trade shows,

- Website, search engine optimisation and web marketing programs.
- Promotional items, sponsorships.

**OPERATIONAL:**

4. **Product:**
    - Description of the product or service.
    - Features and benefits offered relative to competitors.
    - Product development plans to meet changing market demand.

5. **Pricing:**
    - Determined by the market, target market sector, competitors and customer expectations.
    - Market price relative to cost is the primary determinant of profitability for the business.
    - Volume discounts, incentives, variable pricing?

6. **Packaging:**
    Presentation of the product to the consumer:
    - Choices of style, colours and packaging consistent with the corporate image, identity, pricing and performance of the product.
    - Warranty, service, accessories, literature, and regulatory requirements?
    - Retail display, shipping & handling issues?

## *The Four P's of Salesmanship*

1. Patient
2. Persistent
3. Polite
4. Persuasive

*Seven Biggest Mistakes that Entrepreneurs Make*:

1. Too Entrepreneurial
2. Lack of Strategic Direction
3. "Let's do it again!"
4. Focus on Profit
5. Neglecting Key Relationships
6. Poor Marketing and Sales Management
7. Personal Distractions

*How to Avoid Them? The Answer is Balance!*

Avoiding these mistakes requires the entrepreneur and business owner to:

- Balance Entrepreneurial Drive with Planning and Analysis
- Balance Strategic Vision with Operational Detail
- Balance the Logical Head with the Intuitive Heart
- Balance Short-term Profit with Long-term Value
- Balance Personal Priorities with Strategic Objectives.

## *Recommended Reading List and Some Highlights*

In order to help you be better as an entrepreneur, leader and manager, I recommend the following authors for more ideas, information and inspiration. In my opinion, they are among the best at providing thoughtful insights and powerful advice.

I recommend that you make time for them in your own process of continuous learning and improvement. Make your own selection from my list below, then find them online, follow them and read their work.

Here are some of their books and a few memorable quotes:

### Tom Peters
*"There is no more important trait among excellent companies than an action orientation. ... if you've got a major problem, bring the right people together and expect them to solve it. They do, somehow, have the time."*
*"Excellent companies are a vast network of informal, open communications. (Forget the MBA - Masters in Business Administration - and remember the MBWA - Management By Walking Around)"*
***"In Search of EXCELLENCE", 1982***

*"A well-handled problem usually breeds more customer loyalty than you had before the negative incident."*
*"Measure! And reward on the basis of the measures."*
***"Thriving on Chaos", 1987***

### Henry Mintzberg
*"Leadership has pushed management off the map.... Now we are overled and undermanaged."*
*Strategies are not immaculately conceived in detached offices. They are learned through tangible experiences."*
***"SIMPLY MANAGING", 2013.***

## Harvey Mackay

"A goal is a dream with a deadline. Write it down"
"Dig your well before you're thirsty"
"You'll always get the good news; it's how quickly you get the bad news that really counts."
**"SWIM WITH THE SHARKS without Being Eaten Alive", 1988.**

"Do what you love, love what you do and deliver more than you promise."
"You're a lot better off being scared than being bored."
**"BEWARE THE NAKED MAN WHO OFFERS YOU HIS SHIRT", 1990.**

## Jim Collins

"Visionary companies almost religiously preserve their core ideology. Yet, they display a powerful drive for progress that enables them to adapt and change without compromising their cherished core ideals."
"Good enough never is. For these companies the critical question is - How can we do better tomorrow than we did today?"
**"Built to Last", 1994.**

"Good is the enemy of great."
"Confront the brutal facts, yet never lose faith."
**"From Good to Great", 2001**

## Marcus Buckingham & Curt Coffman:

"The one insight that we heard echoed by tens of thousands of great managers: People don't change that much. Don't waste time trying to put in what was left out. Try to draw out what was left in. That is hard enough."
**"First, Break all the Rules", 1999.**

## Seth Godin

*"In advertising... persistence is the secret to success"*
*"In choosing partners remember: Ringo was the luckiest Beatle... a mediocre drummer riding on the backs of three musical geniuses."*
***"The Bootstrapper's Bible", 2004.***

## Guy Kawasaki

*"Build a business to make meaning (the money will follow)."*
*"Have a mantra, not a mission statement."*
*"Advertising is what you say about yourself, PR is what other people say about you. PR is better."*
***"The ART of the START", 2004 and" APE: Author, Publisher, Entrepreneur", 2013.***

## Ben Franklin

*Perhaps best known as an American statesman and scientist, (he signed the Declaration of Independence, flew a kite in a lightening storm, and has his picture on the U.S. $100 bill), Ben Franklin was also a very successful entrepreneur. A printer by trade, he launched several businesses and introduced the concept of franchising to his printing shops. He was successful enough to retire at age forty-two.*

*Following are* **"Ben Franklin's 12 Rules of Management":**

1. Finish better than your beginnings.
2. All education is self education.
3. Seek first to manage yourself, then to manage others.
4. Influence is more important than victory.
5. Work hard and watch your costs.
6. Everybody wants to appear reasonable.
7. Create your own set of values to guide your actions.

8. Incentive is everything.
9. Create solutions for seemingly impossible problems.
10. Become a revolutionary for experimentation and change.
11. Sometimes it's better to do 1001 small things right rather than only one large thing right.
12. Deliberately cultivate your reputation and legacy.

*From "Ben Franklin's 12 Rules of Management" by Blaine McCormick, 2000.*

## Some popular but disappointing reads:

### The E-Myth by Michael Gerber
*Gerber claims he originated the cliché: Work on your business, not in your business. His theme is a useful reminder to develop your business to run without you in it every day.*

### Small Giants by Bo Burlingham
*An interesting study of small eccentric companies that decided to succeed by staying small. The conclusions are a stretch to fit the hypothesis that small is better, but worth reading to remember to build your business for yourself; not to chase some dream of global grandeur.*

## For your Personal Management Issues:

### The 7 Habits of Highly Effective People, Stephen Covey, 1989
*"Begin with the end in mind."*
*"Seek first to understand, then to be understood."*
*More spiritual than you might expect, but some great insights and tools for personal management.*

### *The 8th Habit*, Stephen Covey, 2004
A follow-up book presenting the values of "principle centered" leadership.

### *Awaken the Giant Within*, Anthony Robbins, 1991
"It is the small decisions you and I make every day that create our destinies."

"It is not events that shape my life and determine how I feel or act, it's the way I interpret and evaluate my life experiences."

The original concepts that launched Tony Robbins and the self-help industry.

### *The Intelligent Investor*, Benjamin Graham, 1973, 1984, 2003
From the professor who taught Warren Buffet how to grow his investments to billions. Buffet calls it "By far the best book on investing ever written."

### *The Wealthy Barber* and *The Wealthy Barber Returns*, David Chilton, 1989 and 2011
An easier read than Benjamin Graham and a great basic handbook for personal financial management. Should be required reading for every high school student and every investor paying someone else to manage their money.

Any of these books will help you focus on the fundamentals and achieve more successful approaches to your personal and business growth. It's worth finding the time for them.

And if you have others to recommend I would be pleased to hear from you.

# Thank you for Sharing

*Entrepreneur to Entrepreneur*

This book is dedicated to the principle of sharing among entrepreneurs to help them be better and do better. If you have found it useful, please share the book with other entrepreneurs.

You can also introduce them to Uncle Ralph by reviewing and recommending the book on Amazon.com or your favourite online bookstore. I know I described entrepreneurs as too busy and document-challenged to be interested in reading a book on entrepreneurship, but then I stubbornly wrote this book anyway. So you can help me help them; if I helped you.

And for continuing access to the wisdom of Uncle Ralph you can also link, like or follow Uncle Ralph at these websites:

*Learning Entrepreneurship:*
*www.LearningEntrepreneurship.com*

*Facebook: www.facebook.com/YourUncleRalph*

*LinkedIn: http://ca.linkedin.com/in/delchatterson*

*Twitter: http://twitter.com/Del_UncleRalph*

*Blog for Entrepreneurs:*
*http://learningentrepreneurship.com/learning-blogs/*

I would be pleased to receive your comments and feedback through any of these sites. Part of the process is for me to learn too. Not only to be a better entrepreneur, but to write a better book next time. So don't be shy.

And ***Don't Do It the Hard Way.***

*Your Uncle Ralph*

Del Chatterson

August 2014

# Acknowledgements

*Already dedicated to helping entrepreneurs to do better, I was inspired to write this book by many of the business writers, commentators, journalists and bloggers that I have followed for many years. Most of them are included in my recommended reading list, but a special thank-you to the most impressive and influential: Tom Peters, Harvey Mackay, Henry Mintzberg, Seth Godin, Guy Kawasaki and David Chilton. I acknowledge, appreciate and respect them all.*

*This book has also been made more valuable and useful to entrepreneurs thanks to all the clients, consultants, and business associates that I have worked with during the last thirty years and more. I could not possibly name them all. Some may recognize themselves here even though the characters in the book are only fictional composites of real people. My apologies to anyone who may be less than flattered or if I neglected to tell the best stories and relate all the lessons that we learned together.*

*The quality of this book has also been enhanced by the active support and services offered by my publisher AuthorHouse and Author Solutions LLC.*

*Most important to my completing this project, thank you to my talented and patient wife, Penny Rankin, who supported, encouraged, challenged, edited and improved every revision of the book.*

**Thank you all.**

# The Author

## Your Uncle Ralph
**DEL CHATTERSON is your Uncle Ralph.**

Del is dedicated to helping entrepreneurs around the world to be better and do better.

Del has been successful as an entrepreneur, executive and consultant in manufacturing, distribution, professional services and technology businesses. As an entrepreneur he grew his computer products distribution business from zero to $20 million per year in just eight years. Through his consulting company, DirectTech Solutions, Del provides strategic advice to business owners at all stages: from start-up through the operating and management challenges of achieving sustainable growth and profitability to the exit strategies for management transition and business succession. He applies his expertise to assess business performance and develop strategic plans that achieve higher levels of performance and profitability. His focus is always: *Creative, Practical Business Solutions. Delivered.*

Del graduated as an Engineer and MBA and has lectured on entrepreneurship, financial management and business planning in the business programs at both Concordia and McGill Universities in Montreal. He has given numerous seminars and workshops on business management and entrepreneurship and continues to offer ideas, information and inspiration for entrepreneurs through his Blogs, articles and books under the persona of "Uncle Ralph".

Del offers practical, experienced strategic input and management insights for entrepreneurs worldwide.

In this book he shares his real life stories of entrepreneurship to provide you with new ideas, information and inspiration for your business.

**Learn more at: www.LearningEntrepreneurship.com**

CPSIA information can be obtained at www.ICGtesting.com
Printed in the USA
LVOW11*0743090914

403185LV00002B/12/P